Emotions in Eruption

A poetic journey through life

Barbara Strickland

Copyright © 2017 Barbara Strickland Updated 2018
www.brstrickland.com
Barbara Strickland asserts the moral right to be identified as the author of this work. All rights reserved

No part of this book may be reproduced or transmitted in any form or by any means, electronic or mechanical, including photocopying, recording or any information storage and retrieval system, without prior permission in writing from the author, nor be otherwise circulated in any form of binding or cover other than that in which it is published and without a similar condition including this condition being imposed on the subsequent purchaser.

The names, characters and events portrayed in this publication other than those clearly in the public domain, are fictitious and the work of the author's imagination. Any resemblance to real persons, living or dead is purely coincidental.

ASIN B0761XCBJ3

ISBN 9780648071525

ISBN 9780648071549

Extracts

Unexpected Obsession Copyright © 2017 Barbara Strickland (2016)
Unexpected Passion Copyright © 2017 Barbara Strickland
Emotions in Evolution Copyright © 2018 Barbara Strickland
Author's note: This book was written in Australia and uses British/Australian spelling conventions such as 'colour' instead of 'color', and 'ise' endings instead of 'ize' on words like 'realize'. Some words will also have double ll in its spelling e.g. travel will become travelling.

Images by Kathy Johnson
kathymareejohnson@gmail.com

Cover design and illustration by Christopher Brunton
http://www.cjbrunton.wix.com/brunton-illustration

DEDICATION

To Rose and Vince (my parents),

I wish I had your poems to translate Rose, but reading your writing was an impossible feat. Your scribbling, Vince, was constant, and so is mine. My love for education came from you. Share this with me, it's the best I can do without you here, let you share what you helped create.

To my dearest friend Gail.

I carry the memory of your courage. You are now with someone who will love you and keep you, safe forever. I will miss you always. (Don't worry, we will make it to Norfolk Island, just give me a little more time and keep your fingers crossed)

Acknowledgements

Sean and Kathy, thank you for your help on this project. You have both been incredible. Whatever I have asked, you have done. Your time will come. I know it.

Pat, I couldn't have done this without your help. Julia and Sue, Rosie and Vanessa, you guys are great for listening to me rave, and still supporting me. Thank you to all my family members for not doubting my ability to do this even when I did, and lastly thank you to RS for never letting me give up. You are the wise owl on my shoulder and the butterfly wings that keep me afloat.

Table of Contents

Foreword (2)

REFLECTIONS (Page 4)

Easy Listening (5)
On Thinking Too Much (7)
Lost Art of Friendship (9)
Decision Making (11)
The Buds (13)

HUMAN CONTACT (Page 14)

Nobody Is Perfect (I love you) (15)
Birthing (17)
Butterfly Child (19)
Binary Opposition (21)
Players (23)
Distractions of the Heart (25)
Lucid Tranquillity (27)
The Cabbage Patch Doll (30)

REALITY (Page 31)

Forgotten Magic (32)
Spring Blossoms (33)
Choosing Blindness (34)
Competition (36)
Imagine (38)
Dreaming (40)
The Stubborn Heart (42)
Romantic Fantasy (43)
Don't Shut the Door (44)

The Dreamer Never Dies (46)
Semantics (48)
A Simply Stunning Slaughter (49)
The Extension (51)
Soul-Kissed (Nico's Lament) (53)
Ignorance (55)

SORROW (Page 58)

Self-Portrait (59)
Night and Day (60)
Anorexic Purging (61)
Impossible Lover (Nico's Ode to Lia) (63)
Invisible (65)
Depressed – To Be or Not to Be (67)
Addictive Patterns (69)
Self-Harm (71)
Sad Movies Make Me Cry (73)
This Last Episode (75)
The Waiting Game (77)
Desert Living (79)
Broken Promises (81)
Monsoonal Madness (83)
Petulance (85)
Immobilisation (86)
Deprivation (88)
Desperation (90)

CROSSROADS (Page 92)

Oops, I Messed Up Again (93)
I Am Not in Love (95)
Intersection (98)
Midnight Deception (100)
Indifference (101)

Adulthood (103)
Change of Life (105)
Missing the Boat (107)

NEXT (Page 109)

Seasons in Turmoil (110)
Belonging (1112)
At the End (114)

PEOPLE AND WINE (Page 116)

People are like fine wine (117)
The Adventurer (118)
The Pacifist (118)
The Sensualist (119)
The Pleasure Seeker (119)
The Thinker (120)
The Conversationalist (120)

CHERRY BLOSSOM (Page 121)

Memories from a Japanese Trip (122)

From the author (124)
Book/About the author (125)
Unexpected Obsession extract (126)
Unexpected Passion extract (184)
Emotions in Evolution (202)

Welcome

to
Emotions

FOREWORD

Putting pen to paper, or rather fingers to a keyboard can be quite confronting. Automatically there is a suggestion that the words matter. They do. Your words should matter. Words lend strength and give voice. Silence holds us back.

I wrote this because in times of crisis I give myself a voice. At times that voice may seem exaggerated, emotional, a little bizarre, or left field but it is real. It exists. I cope by putting and yes at times *over putting* (over sharing perhaps) things down on paper. I have been lost, lonely and unhappy. I have been delighted, dazzled and elated. It is the nature of the world and its people to feel emotions, both good and bad.

However, when the feelings are not pleasant the tendency is to hide, to believe we are alone and foolish in our thoughts and reactions. For me sharing in the form of writing, any kind, helps me find perspective. We are supposed to hide the negative and thus feel guilty because in sharing we believe we burden. I disagree. By speaking we face our fears, and if we are fortunate, we find understanding. In speaking up we are seeking a solution. We burden when we hide. That battle fatigues our soul.

Sometimes the instinct to survive is shrouded in semantics, both for speaker and the hearer of the language for though love is supposed to be unconditional, the reality of life intrudes. The expectancy is to be strong, to be positive and to perform accordingly. In theory it sounds good and I wish it was possible to obliterate negative thoughts and actions. It's not. It is the contrariness of human beings.

The price is a fragile butterfly that emerges and doesn't know how to fit into the limitations on offer. Without a leaf of light on which to rest the butterfly will falter and the delicate flavour of finely spun wings will dissipate into the breeze and be gone. We need to be exactly who we are, and not someone others believe we should be, or we risk becoming a creature folding its wings and becoming an unseen whisper.

But, words can bring us freedom from pain, and unfold the wings to fly again another day. I would have perished without my ability to express my thoughts. I don't need any one to approve them or to like how they appear on the page, but my hope is one word resonates and then someone out there knows they are not alone.

Barbara Strickland

Don't hurt the butterfly, it will die soon enough

Reflections

Do you see only what you think is there?

Easy Listening

*I remember when it was all laid out
what role to take.
You want to shout
it was simple.*

*Waiting to be told
what clothes, what food, when, where
because otherwise was bold.
It was simple.*

*Directed how to achieve
grasping for prizes was controlled
but easy if you wanted to believe –
it was simple.*

*Life demands choices,
cryptic variants of
different paths and loud voices
searching for what is simple.*

Longing deep for normality,

the memories seem safe.
Age brings a strange formality
asking was simple ever there?

On Thinking Too Much

*How to make it stop
so that it recedes, disappears,
this constant turning of thoughts
that haunt me, even in
those precious moments
when joy, exists?
I did not want to feel.
I was right. But, the
need to take a chance
was stronger than
I expected and so I entered
that frightening world.
No peace there because
I was right.
And now pain pierces painfully.
I am scarred, bruised and
lonely when before I was*

just alone.

I was wrong to believe in

fairy tales, and white horses, and

handsome heroes.

Now with cold certainty

I must learn to forget

how to read.

Lost Art of Friendship

Ethereal magic.

Substantial.

A butterfly kiss,

so light, that

even to breathe

becomes a dare.

Warmth, spreading and

touching my often cold,

and always bleeding heart.

Overwhelming,

so that at the fall

of darkness there is

an abundance of light

to relinquish the ever

present pain beyond

my elusive control.

Are you real?

Are you a dream sequence?

Is that your

voice, or my mind?

Whatever, whoever,

you are the living

proof of the meeting

of souls.

You are my friend

when I take the time

to see you.

Decision Making

I don't want to.

Instead

I feel the urge to

rant and rave.

I know I have to.

Instead

I feel the urge to

quietly cave.

I've been dealt a card.

It's far too hard.

I close my eyes

and hope

I wake up wise.

I have seen the

echoed smile reflected,

in a happiness file.

I carefully remove
all the shiny blades,
sighing as the
anger fades.

The Buds

Rustling winds call my name

and awaken me to play the game.

I slowly dress

and to myself confess

though the rules seem less,

nothing seems the same.

Whirling wheels of distant blame

reluctantly decide to claim

the fading lights

of long-lost flights,

and unwanted plights

leading back to covert shame.

To the recesses of yesterday

I banish all dead flowers.

Let them rest where they may

and allow new buds their untried powers.

Human Contact

Pieces on boards are moved by humans.

Nobody is Perfect (*I love you*)

Often, I wonder why

you have the power

to make cry.

The sudden silence of my heart

understands,

knows, all

you do is simply thoughtless.

Sometimes fine,

sometimes cold

and cruel

so that an oozing occurs.

There is bleeding as

the sharp knife, you plunge.

The deep and sudden penetration

is bitter and I find it

hard to remember that

I wanted and needed you.

Never did I dream

that this kind of love could

be a torment.

In growing up

the distance must have shifted.

Whereas before your childhood needs

tore at my core,

I find now you rip me into shreds,

and I have not the energy

to repair the threads.

Yet I am amazed at what you can do.

That glimpsed rich smile

directed my way,

has so much power

to make me say,

it does not matter those things

I filed,

for after all you are

and always will be

my beloved born child.

Birthing

A small vibration builds

slowly, piercingly pinching

and penetrating like a summer insect

that at dusk must come out

to show the night as an

imperfect medium

contrasting

with bitingly bitter stinging sensations

to the sweetness of the sun filled days.

A constant running of close

together eruptions, erosions

and errors of nature which

display a natural process as an

imperfect medium

contrasting

the truisms handed down since the

beginning of time and human evolution.

A final cutting edge of sans pity

statements screaming sinfully silent

and showing only at the

almost merciless end

that the imperfect medium is

in contrast to

what you imagined

a long yearned for

and deeply desired creation.

Butterfly Child (Lia's song)

Because of you

I feel the lightest touch of soft satin wings.

I see the rainbow in all things.

If I could contain you upon my hand,

you would be as delicate as grains of sand.

Finely formed, reflecting the glimmer of summer shine,

sweet of temper and pure of soul,

such a strong straight line.

You are the best of me.

You are the gift only of

the Butterfly that I am and so

you are the softness of my wings, and

the rainbow colours that I wear I

bequeath to you because in

you they flourish.

And

so, I think it only fair to for you to know

when I am long gone from you and

you see a butterfly passing by,

that

it will be me that you do not see

and it will be me reminding you, that

every day in every way

I loved you more

than I knew to say.

Binary Opposition

We were a union made to explore.

One heartbeat,

strong and sure.

A physicality to be admired,

a truth of mind and core.

One of us dissipated,

melted, dissolved but essence

remained to taunt that one of us

left alone to

inhabit that secret place.

Made to stay there,

alone, afraid

and in the dark,

ignored, and deplored I

hoped to escape your mark.

Shuddering, I accepted you were

ingrained. You colour my blood.
You are the language that explains me
and you have the right not
to be starved by my frightened soul.

Come, take your light.
Join me now
for we are meant to be
and this time I will allow
your Growth, and I will
not call your goodness weak.
And I will not be afraid to love
completely, unconditionally
with all that I am
for I am tired
and can no longer
play the game
on this broken stage
by myself.

Players

Chance meeting.

Pleasant, nice,

but safety rules.

Pieces are moved forward.

Silent pawns stand unafraid.

This is only an interlude.

Sudden tension.

Fearful, unbearable.

The Queen is in check.

She remains unthreatened

but knows the game has changed.

There is need for reflection.

The King glides forward,

demanding, powerfully intent.

The Queen is aloof.

Uncertainty brings sacrifices
and the board is now alien.
The precipice is jagged.

She alone must decide.
She alone moves forward.
Danger pervades but
the prize is golden, attainable
and worth the risk.
This is more than an interlude.

The King senses capitulation.
The King moves.
The King purposefully turns.
The King is not ready for veracity.

He moves away callously.
The Queen dies.

Distractions of the Heart

Abandonment of all those dreams,
concentration instead on schemes.
Forget the longing and heart-felt yearning,
the future beckons and the wheels are turning.
But I whisper to the wind distracted,
maybe this time I will not be compacted.
Liar, Liar, inside your mind you shout,
this is not the end of the drought.
You are hoping,
you are moping,
you are not ready for another coping.

This time it will be different,
you are not swimming against the current.
You came to this with some insight.
You fought a brave and gallant fight.
But I whisper to the wind in sweet rapture,

will loving slowly, prevent the fracture?
Liar, Liar, inside your mind you shout.
Do not go there and forget to doubt.
You are running.
He is cunning.
You are not ready for another gunning.

What do I do then with this distraction?
Do I turn away from the attraction?
And so, I do my whispering to the wind,
and hope with all my heart
this time, he will not rescind.

I am a fool to make this admission.
I cannot help myself, I want remission.

Lucid Tranquillity

I hear You.
But, those voices,
those escalating influences
call me and I falter.
Your echo is far better.
It triggers a spiritual spiral
towards a lucidity
so often escaping my notice.

To be calm,
to be tranquil shudders
me into splintered fragile
snowflakes of melting
emotional madness.
I know I am the creator.
I know my power but
still I am hostage to

silvered slides of
syntax makers, who want
their universal limitations
to rule supreme
over others, others
who do not understand
the glory of manifestation
and sadly, cowardly
bend to the collector.

I am left frozen,
the withered wraith
of a broken spirit
bereft of presence,
a diminished aura
of splattered, faded and
crumbling colours
never to blend.
I hear You.

I know what You say.

Be patience generous,

for I am

only now unfurling

from

my embryonic

prison.

The Cabbage Patch Doll

I saw it first as small and sweet.

I saw it then get on its feet.

Giant steps, giant words.

The doll-like creature

had an adult-like feature.

I cried and cried

and thought I'd died.

Giant steps, giant words,

until the human hands

back from foreign lands

opened up, to reveal,

what suddenly I could feel.

The cabbage patch now was full.

I let myself enjoy the pull.

Now I watch the dolls at play

and happily, keep the tears at bay.

Reality

We begin, we end. We can only hope the in-between is not left blank.

Forgotten Magic

In the music of your silence
comes the perfect peace as
green and grasping you
touch my soul with your
magical root-centred existence.

The darkness you inhabit
is dense and full-bodied, holding
fears in perspective, for
underneath hungrily avid is
Life in rainbow-coloured glory.

I may never get the
chance to see your
undoubted splendour, for I live
ensnared by different choices.
Nevertheless, I hope.

Spring Blossoms

Pretty blossoms to be
adored with pleasure.
Drawn, pulled from the deepest
part of the earth to grow,
to prove beauty is really
from within. For are not
the trunk and branches ugly in the
winter frozen chill?

Delicate, the softest of colour
combinations, barely there
and yet such a bold fashion
statement to represent the coming of
a new season,
and a new beginning.
I wish we could
be so, simply beautiful.

Choosing Blindness

The music flows.

Sometimes smooth,

an uninterrupted path

into the soul.

Generous acceptance may allow

completed entry, to make the whole.

Fearful hesitancy, unspoken barriers,

control graceful gratitude

and destroy the magic

of the pleasant interlude.

The loser moves silently along

severely clever, not glimpsing joy.

Value lost, ignored, unseen, and

agonizingly, a deflected ploy.

Did you know, during that endless search,

you alone held the key?

The music will always flow

but not for you, afraid to know.

Competition

In the market place of
sheer commodity
you wonder fiercely
about your oddity.
Exclusivity is your sole aim.
But, the playing board denotes
a violent game.

Questions fly with deadly speed.
Voracity must rise to meet the need.
You cry choose me, choose me
and have no patience then
to wait and see, and
life revolves around the passion
that kills, destroys and
mutilates compassion.

You need to stay alert to read the news.

You must be on top to get the clues.

Those paradigms are flying fast

and you need to be the first, not last.

Open eyes and listen well.

Prepare to run upon the bell.

Imagine

*Peaceful thoughts and
an ability to get through the
Day and Night without the
constant distraction of buts
and dreaded ifs and maybes
of the so-called normal life.
We search the world.
We search new things
to do and make and
we look for hobbies,
we try the different.
We change the people
in our lives
and still we cannot find.
It is somewhere out there
eluding us, taunting us and we
weep. We let anger rule*

and frustration reign

when all the time

it is right here.

It is not the geography

that gives us tranquillity

but rather the acceptance of

ourselves.

Dreaming

If I could manifest my thoughts
to you
upon the breeze they would float
and sit
until you allowed that moment
when
absorption occurs, and they melt
inside your mind.
You would take them with a
puzzled distraught frown,
your internals turning, churning,
thrashing up and down
and you would know deep in
that silent waiting part
that it is a waste of time
to be so mindlessly far apart.

But this is reality, a test of faith and give.

And right this minute, you are far too human,

to let my manifestations in

and let them live.

I will wait, I know you.

You will come to me.

I have waited this long,

I will wait a little bit longer

for where I belong.

The Stubborn Heart

Every time I allow my heart
to open like the proverbial door
I also choose a poison dart
and engage in hurt a little more.

It's time to stop not start
to protect that tiny internal core.
Acknowledgement in blood
must be minimal
to prevent that dreaded flood.
Sad cannot be subliminal.

Black, iron cast impenetrable door
Where heavy handles block my power
The heart rules less, the head rules more
And my face becomes dismally and forever dour.

Romantic Fantasy

One look and it seems

enough.

One touch and the magician

lives.

No doubts,

no insecurities.

Joy reigns.

Bubbling infectious domino

effect.

My pillows hit the wooden floor.

My mobile calls my name.

Ha! I was dreaming.

What a damned shame!

Don't Shut the Door

I tried so hard.

I tried so long.

I turned each card.

I heard each song.

Every single time

I sought the rhyme.

You know the one.

It begins the fun.

I ran towards the road

breaking every traffic code.

I ran towards the church steeple

praying for less elusive people.

I ran back home,

too tired now to roam,

too many answers yet to find,

too many faces so unkind.

I still had hope

and the ability to cope

until I slammed

into the door.

You know the one.

It lands you on the

floor

and stops the fun.

The Dreamer Never Dies

Again, I listen.
Again, I am a prisoner
of that cunning heart
that refuses time and time again
to stop believing in those
dreadful fairy tales
that reek of love and romance
and goodness and happy endings.
Traitor, I call that beating organ
that has no ability to
stop and think what it will
mean to bleed. For God's sake the
fool forgets it is a main
supply of life force and
to bleed once more will evaporate
the last vestige of hope,
a vampire death where I walk

but my life is empty.

It was the music.

It drew out possibilities I had

long ago put in a box.

I really should stop playing the music.

Semantics

Solitary is being alone.
Different to
being lonely.
Alone is a choosing to be.

Confusion so often becomes
interchangeable and so we move
between two worlds, always afraid
to know the consequences, and
making choices from avoidance until
reality comes your way
in silken softness you
cruelly dissect, and the pieces stay
in your heart and your soul
and you drown
and you become lonelier.
Alone is so much better.

A Simply Stunning Slaughter

Breathe gently, move slowly.
The floor below is fragile glass.
Smile, drift and freely float
and let the music dancing, entice.

The mice are handsome.
The pumpkin is rich and golden.
Your clothing bold and daring
and your slippers concreted to the ground.

Enjoy the magical world appearing,
and be radiantly enmeshed in moonlight.
You are the soft sensation of a cloud.
You are the warming hearth where dreams exist.

Defenceless then,
you become the hopeless victim to

the never imagined, simply stunning

slaughter of your mind.

The Extension

I listen for the sound.

I wait for that light,

to flash blood.

I have to answer, now

before

it all becomes a flood.

A finger takes it to

Person A,

another one becomes

Person B.

Each time, exciting and new,

not

that I ever see.

My life is a reflection.

I live

in the in-between.
I hear everything but
I live,
where I can't
be seen.

The solid black gets
human contact.
It survives to feel
the grasp of fingers,
the touch of skin.
Should I envy
that unliving being?
Yes, of course.
It has no ability to sin.

Soul-Kissed (Nico's Lament)

Awareness so profound

I tremble when you are around.

Adaption so intense

that my intelligence makes no sense.

You live inside my head.

You will live until I am dead.

Chemistry is just a word

to minimise what has occurred.

I bent and kissed your mouth

and to my heart your taste went south.

It fooled me into thinking

love would not cloud my sinking.

I thought I could just stimulate

returning later to manipulate.

Selfishness drove my need

as my ego fought to feed.

What we got was so much more
than I ever dreamed to explore.
I think on reflection we soul-kissed.
Fearfully I brutally dismissed.
Then I discovered I was blind
for soul-kissers cannot unbind.
We are forever forged and fused
and those who watch are well amused.
I thought I played a mortal game
with courage then to take the blame.
But when you soul-kiss you become a fool
and fall into that deep and endless pool
where no escape will let you free
where no peace will ever be
for you must pay with deep regret.
Soul-kissing is not something you can forget.

Ignorance

Visions

constantly

turning over

so that the mind

never sleeps.

Where, why,

what purpose?

Admit and acknowledge

justifications that the

insecurity of the reality in

comparison to comfort is

only a perception.

Interpretations

so constant they

become a bible.

*A religion then
so deeply ingrained
it becomes disdain,
contempt, and
a critique of all
outside limits of the
narrow globe we live in.*

*Warmth, disappearing.
Frigidity settling in and
creating divisions. Spheres
becoming smaller,
disintegrating
into waxen dust.
Plastic missing
the vital irritation
cannot be ignored.
A death of the soul is
he who is there*

with no one to care.

Sorrow

Sadness is just a state of mind. Change it.

Self-Portrait

Intricate patterns of clear

interwoven with butterflies and

tulips, the stain of reality for

the mind, represented.

Colours, beautiful, bold

and catching the sight but not the eye

for the eye will recognise fragility

but sight will see stained glass.

Delicate, easily shattered.

Fragmented into the mixed

tiny, shiny pieces that can be

subtly shaped to appear

meaningful, but are in truth

deceptively inclined to

hide what is after all

damaged goods and broken glass,

no matter the fixation of Glory.

Night and Day

I love you.

I fear you.

When I am there,

you are here.

When I am here

you disappear.

An illusion

to soul give?

In forever,

can I believe?

There is light

and then darkness

when you leave

my side and I discover,

the deepest part of me you

sever.

Anorexic Purging

Mindless chasing of rainbows
putting true existence in doubt.
But, does not reality reign ruthless and
often at the cost of clarity?
Is this the only way?
Desperate alienation
of soul, and mind?
Where is inner peace?
I hunger for it and
throw it back. I feed
and cannot be fed.
I starve myself with greed.
I purge, I eat, I purge
but never does the balance
I seek show itself.
There is nothing of me
but human, unsightly flesh.

I hate it. Make it disappear.

Impossible Lover *(Nico's Ode to Lia)*

Fragile in your

steel frame.

Surprisingly passionate,

so unexpected, so intense,

so boundless and

God forgive me

so vulnerable.

Intelligent in your

eggshell abode.

Surprisingly addictive,

so true, so vital,

so focused and

God forgive me

so ill chosen.

A loving heart,

in this heartless world.

I am forever

remorseful.

Life toyed, played a confusingly cruel and disenchanting game.

Invisible

Mine is,

a loneliness

of the soul.

Part of, and

apart from,

I move in the reality

of dreams

where everything is

not what it seems.

Fragmented,

mosaic.

A puzzle within a

puzzle, the

scattered pieces of

life move into

irrational gleams

*of somewhat distant
unsynchronized scenes.
My choice,
based on my perceived
needs and desire to
fight the unearthly fire.*

*Destructive,
cleansing extremities
of my nature.
Fragmented mosaic
tiles of history
denied existence
with ego selfishness.
In sleep perhaps
a union of small pieces
where everything is
just what it seems.*

Depressed – To Be or Not To Be

Distanced from the

Detail overview.

Deceptively quiet inside.

Deadly loud outside.

Do get out of bed.

Do not break this stillness.

Directions from the head,

Distractions from the heart.

Duty is calling.

Death calls louder.

Decisions

Distress

Dignity is pretence.

Disaster is reality.

Do pull yourself together.

Do enter the pain realm.

Diligence

Digression

Do I want to be good?

Do I have the energy?

Do I want answers?

Do I know the questions?

Depression

Do I start the process?

Does the process start me?

Do I care?

I need to stop and think.

Addictive Patterns

Desires circle in the

mind,

that void of brainless

thought,

never learning until

the ending is confused

and the starting line

is never crossed.

Days cycling by like

metres

and metres of environmental

sameness,

never ending until

the beginning is confused

and the finishing line

is never reached.

Fragile heart now,

Pieces of glass.

Splintered.

Shattered

and thrown in

so many directions

that the home is

displaced and

both beginning and ending

have co-inhabited

and

there is no place to go.

No beginning – you no longer dare.

No ending – you were never there.

Self-Harm

I just tried again.

Don't bother with towels or cloths.

There was no blood.

unless you count the

liquid spillage that

tears bring even if

they are dry-eyed delivered.

It was far more, subtle,

more personal,

more painful and severely unseen.

Unless of course there

were witnesses to see.

You believe in Him,

The Being above,

Who knows all,

*Who watches helpless but
with desperate hope,
desperate belief, and
desperate hard-won faith
and you finally ask
the question.
Is this the last time?*

It wasn't. It isn't.

Sad Movies Make Me Cry

Cold and calculating.

My God, that is fascinating.

Ambivalent, or belligerent?

How exciting? How very different?

Time to laugh, time to smile,

emotions coming out file by file.

Dear, that is so very bad.

I think that character is quite mad.

Please do not let him die.

Oh goodness me, what a terrible lie.

They have come so far. Do they have to part?

So much to sacrifice,

for the sake of Art?

Sad movies make me cry.

Reality only makes me sigh.

Sad movies make me feel

and forget the real.

Sad movies fade away, but

life is here.

Every single day.

I think that I will leave

the TV on

even if others

frown upon

the box where I behold

the watching of the world, unfold.

I would rather watch than participate.

I would rather watch than activate.

This Last Episode

Not the last be sure
but this one, effectively chilling
dampening the glow of
soul-reached compromise
and bringing back the
battle-fixed arena where
fear is constant and
trust the fearful enemy.

Amazing behaviour.
Unnecessary, taunting, painful
when belief in magic
is much sweeter.
But, and but is forcefully
if frantically in existence, the
true sorrow is found to have
shifted from you, yourself,

*to them, themselves, who
live without the vestige of
delicious hope within.
Fools! It transcends
what is,
to what may still be.*

The Waiting Game

A somewhat intricate beauty

fills my vision and

it disturbs my tired body.

The scene blurs, merges

becoming distorted between the

world that is and the world

I want it to be.

I long for the

carousel to stop.

It is internal and

relentless in its turning.

It prods, pulls and punishes.

It questions, raises doubts.

The destination is unknown

and beyond the knowledge

of the me that has

become the me,

that is the now.

I see it clearly.

That resting place

I long have searched,

and know it is real,

know it exists.

Have I been there

and missed it all?

What is imagination?

What is need?

What is longing?

What is real?

It is my Carousel.

I press the button.

Desert Living

I hate the way nobody sees,

nobody listens.

Eyes are for viewing,

taking in the tiny drops of

life

revolving,

evolving,

and happening

constantly around us

except in this silent

wasteland of nothingness

where a crowded visual is

a stretch of

empty sand.

Ears are for hearing

the sounds that

rustle, slowly feeding

awareness of

life

revolving.

evolving,

and happening

constantly around us,

except in this busy

expansion of nothingness

where a noisy wind is

an expanse of

empty clouds.

Why so blind?

Why so deaf?

I am desperate.

I dehydrate

a little more each day.

Broken Promises

Trappings of gold and white
inhabiting four walls,
sharing surface things until
you wonder what is real
and
what is not,
what is enough
and
what is social illusion
and
dictionary definition
totally out of context
with satin sheets
and lonely nights
even when
a breath away.
And,

a lifetime goes by

and

you are still waiting

to

have it made clear

but

the book is jargonised,

a dichotomy of rules

and

you are language-less

enough already

with

all you have so naively given.

And,

you wake up

and

finally, thankfully,

you are living by yourself,

alone.

Monsoonal Madness

A drop. A drop.

A tiny little drop.

It went away.

It had nothing

whatever to say.

When it came again,

it was barely there

but some heard

despite pitifully

whispered sounds.

Later some called it

a bombardment

of strange ideas

and burning tears.

It left for unknown places.

It was only, drops of water.

Why then did it feel like slaughter,

a mindless destruction

of pitiful faces?

Petulance

What is it?
A mind thing or
the invisible wound on
the abstract heart that
foolishly allows entry.

What does it do?
Travels insidiously in
the veins of emotions to
mark territory signs at
the deepest root-base.

Who does it?
You! And all those
others who savagely
partake in the ego dubious
thrill of soul demise.

Immobilisation

I have seen the Light
but I feel cold.
I have seen the Dark
but I am far too warm
to find comfort
or peace.

Immobile to move forward
and unable to go back
I have found a purgatory of
day-to-day existence.
It is not living.
It is immobilising.

Momentary joys are followed
by the hollowness of
confusion.

Where do we find the wheels?
Where are my roller blades?
Where is my vehicle of escape?

This path is hazardous.
The road is badly concreted
and full of holes, tumours, dark
and pitted and when it ends
I find the familiar pattern
inside my head.

Navigation is possible.
Maps are found
in plentiful array.
Diagrams help plot
the path. Unfortunately
I am immobile by choice.

Deprivation

Can this continue?
This lack of breath,
this frozen state?

Yet it does.
And days go by
and no one and nothing
notices blood in the snow.
It hurts the most
what others miss.
A black hole of tears
never cried because
the Abyss is huge
and the pain voracious
and there is no way to demand
attention because the oxygen is almost gone.

I can't breathe in

and I am afraid to breathe out

and I don't know what is in-between.

The process of life is missing

and despite the savage suction of sound

there is only silence to hear me.

Desperation

Does no-one care

about

loneliness and despair?

I am fading into the night

lacking memories of the light.

Cold, the icicles form around me,

a door without a key.

They stand silent witnesses

as I mourn, sad,

frightenedly forlorn.

I feel buried.

I am trapped.

All my energy has been sapped.

The hurt has changed to deadly.

It has become bitterness friendly.

I am now afraid of the dark.

I can't rid myself of its mark.

I know if I try,
I can switch on that light.
What if I prefer to die
to escape this confusing,
overwhelming,
painful,
insight.

Crossroads

I don't know which path to take.

Do you?

Oops, I Messed Up Again

Today I fell and
turned back time.
Pushing, battling to
move on, I tired. And,
yearned for mediocrity.

The past pulls tightly
at the subconscious mind.
It has already failed to
move on because
it knows only mediocrity.

The penalty of femaleness,
to fear the independence of
aloneness.
My heart breaking,
my will forsaking,

my body shaking

with determination,

I try to stand up.

The floor is slippery.

A change of shoes may be in order.

I Am Not in Love

Inexplicable, to feel this way

when the mind is

screaming rationalise,

conclude, then exclude.

This obsession that is now

a point of no return and

a cause to bleed until

even the most ravenous of

vampire is bloated and

ready for true death, forsaking

the pretence of living that

is excitement only in brief

suckling moments of warmth

leading to a climax that

is explosive but too

quickly gone to ever

know what reality is.

*I am shattered, broken
and this painful human
condition that is prized
so highly has become
the nightmare of dreams.
and I battle to justify
existence, and I battle
to breathe, and I battle to
believe in even myself
for myself could not
hold the lover, and
even more could not hold
the humanity of
acknowledgement and
yet I called it love
and believed it special.
My ability to think was
pathetically caught up
with the stereotype.*

I am not in love, for love is just a word.

Intersection

Did I choose you?

Did you happen?

Does it matter?

Turn right, go left.

Straight ahead is better

but the potholes

are constant

and the scarring,

bloody brutal.

Going back is

now impossible.

Maybe just a little?

Or maybe just a lot?

What do I choose now?

Or, do I let it happen?

Why is the road so hard?

Can someone help me?

Is there a map?

A diagram to direct me?

I need a hand.

I can't do this alone.

Moonlight Deception

Sharply defined you tease my mind.

Distraught with fear I shed a tear.

Inside my heart your words do dart.

I know your name but are you still the same?

Does the word trust taste like rust?

Does the moonlight lie and let the sunlight die?

Are you the link so I can think?

When the madness drifts, will there be rifts?

I am so afraid that myself I cannot upbraid.

This fear is so great it will not abate.

Is it you and the things you do?

Or is it me who has lost the key?

Indifference

I see it all.
Those man-made memories
where joyful explosions of
emotion brings tears,
and laughter.
A reptilian warmth.

I call it orgasm.
It may be real but
it is a fraction only
of the moment that
pleasured time pretends
to us, is more.

I am the frosted ice
of man-made memories
where painful explosions

of emotions bring tears.
Sorrow,
the silken slippery price.

It is an orgasm.
It is a whole lifetime
spotted by blood that
is the moment
pleasure deceives us as
meaningful.

I think I would rather
indifference.
I am weak though
and I will
succumb to hope and
those disruptions will
fragment me till
I am gone.

Adulthood

I grew up today.
I saw truth.
Your eyes are not so nice
and I had to protect
myself.
Truth is truth
but in your being
truth is a lie.
I could have
gone on forever but
I am not yet weak enough
to surrender to the
Cynical Cyclone and let it
destroy all chances that
hope is worth fighting for
and necessary to
my survival.

*I win, you lose but
I am now a grown up,
and my heart may
bleed for you but,
I see it now.*

I see what is.

Change of Life

I am afraid.
I tremble and cry
silent tears.
I have not the
courage to admit
to those around me that
I am unhappy and so
very sad.

I am powerless to
make changes.
I want to, and
perhaps in knowing that
and in noticing
others too feel this way
I can be less self-indulgent
and leave selfishness behind.

It is selfish to live inside

myself and

deceptive to

think that it

protects me to be

silent.

Missing the Boat

I am an amoeba.
I divide the centuries and flow
in bits and pieces and I multiply
until not even I know
where I go

The human heart,
the physical shape.
The strange complicated
human brain
takes over justifying,
rationalising
till I lose the will
to just explain.

Perplexed, in total confusion
I meander down so many roads

that push and probe at me,

and take me aside.

Good paths, pot-holed paths,

and indifferent ones

causing so much surprise

I am still alive.

Thus, I dissolve

into the scattered parts of

divisions, greedily growing,

exploding into nations.

Wondering always

What is the outcome?

Will there be fruition

from these creations?

Next

The end of the old, and the beginning of the unknown.

Seasons in Turmoil

What happened to Spring?

When did the Summer go?

What was I doing,

to miss the arrival?

How didn't I know?

Autumn,

the best of all.

Autumn,

varied, full of sweet reflections,

and bitter moments and yet

Autumn,

the best of all, magic because

aging, when the process is styled,

has dignity, and the slide from

gold to brown is

a caressing, warming chill

heralding acceptance and

becoming a mentor to all

the things to come, and

the mentor becomes a

friend to all the things left behind.

Every day reaches out

to the brightest stars and their soft,

shining, sprinkled delicate dust adds

a hopeful flavour to the menu the

Universe is still serving.

I am not impatient for the Winter.

I wait, knowing I will find

the comfort of blankets.

Why not?

I bought them a long time ago.

Belonging

Sensations tearing at the internal being.

Connections slow and strong.

Piercing sounds pushed aside.

Deep entrenchment that

calls me back

against my will

to a time and place.

Disparity of skin and speech.

Forceful reality thrown into existence.

Shadows propositioning.

Hidden intricate attachment

that I escaped and

that now ensnares me

to the time and place.

I carry the inhabited weight of

the centuries on my shoulders.

A privilege enveloping and

making me forever

Who

and

What

I am – my birthright.

And at the End

What is there?

A cessation

of the turbulent thinking,

of the mind travelling,

of the constant thoughts

taking me to places

where I never really wanted

to go, not then

and certainly not now.

Is there a nirvana,

of constant achievement

of confused cycles

of random rationality

giving life to individuality

I never really wanted?

Most assuredly not back then

when the energy was higher,

and certainly not now.

Were there choices?

Was there a sanity

of planned purpose?

Did I fail to understand?

Did I choose ambiguous words?

Did I confuse meanings somehow?

Is that why, even now,

there are still steps,

endless, endless steps to climb?

I am more accepting of love and

thankfully I am closer to above.

I had to understand though

to be a little further from below.

People and Wine

ial *Characters we meet*

People are like a fine wine

The barrel chosen,
picked with care, and
perceptive knowledge
lovingly houses and
caresses the aging of
no longer
flowing contents.

The rich, unprocessed,
in-depth blend
becomes
the individual housing
the unique flavoured
palette
of personality.

Blood-based liquid
drawn from nature's
precious gift and
human sweat combines
with time
to house
treasured and distinctive taste.

Meet some of my companions

The Adventurer

*Andiamo says the voice inside
for the new is waiting to be
tried.
Andiamo means to move and go,
extend our palate with a balanced
flow.
A hint of danger, rustic paths to explore.
Lethally addictive bouquet so we want
more.*

The Pacifist

Dolce, sweet, a throat balm.
Silent, sliding delicately spreading
calm.
Delicious, slowly warming fire
partnering the crisp and tart without the
ire
Purity of colour flowing slow.
Refined, pacifying, and worth the
know.

The Sensualist

Amore, the ultimate aim,
is sinfully selfish in the goal for
fame.
Full-bodied, fleshy perfumes fall,
floating, savouring, lost in the
call.
Sensuality oozes, the throat swallows.
Amore in the lingering completion that
follows.

The Pleasure Seeker

Man, and wine join and become one.
Desire rules so let the experience be
done.
Feel, smell and taste is prime,
and the actions a mouth-filling
crime.
Velvet feel, intoxicating aroma
and sinful need leads to a heavenly

coma.

The Thinker

Indulgent thoughts will prepare
as the rustic and robust have nostrils flare.
Complexity encourages and moves
as we filter earth and fruit into oaky grooves.
The mind is ready to stop.
Bring on bottle and a glass; time to prop.

The Conversationalist

Conversing is an exquisite share
for those with aged knowledge to bare.
Discussions will flow as the bottle sits elegant and ripe with fragrances it emits.
No educational surprises here.
Expecting the best brings satisfaction not fear.

CHERRY BLOSSOMS

Haiku memories from a Japanese Trip

white mountain calls

resolutions in misted ice on lava

fierce movement

beauty in silent idle hands

rippling earth

busy lives encased in concreted skyline glory

honour flutters softly on the harsh past

peaceful warrior heart

smiling warmth abides
hot embers reach limits
cleansing fire rebuilds

differences fade
West and East
misted skins dazzle

fast lane hunger runs
timeless history ambles
true essence prevails

cherry pink blossom
blood on white petals
joyous harmony

From the Author

For your reading pleasure, and a change of pace, I have enclosed the beginning chapters of my novel **Unexpected Obsession, Book 1** from **The Unexpected Series**.

I am also including a brief unedited extract and introduction to Lexi and Ricardo who take centre stage in **Book 2, Unexpected Passion**. I am working hard to have this out early 2019.

If you have read this far then you have finished reading **Emotions in Eruption** and most likely have mixed reactions. I don't blame you. But this was a project I needed to do. I am so grateful you have taken the time and spent money on something I have written. I have a small favour to ask of you before you leave. Would you please consider leaving a review? Be as honest as you wish. I learn from you.

For Indie authors reviews can make the difference between success and financial solvency or nothing. **Word of mouth is an author's best friend.** Just a brief word and a rating left at Amazon will truly make that difference.

Thank you,
Barbara Strickland.

I have no plans for a newsletter at this stage but will post news and updates through my Amorina Rose's blog posts or on my home page. Both are found on my official website:
www.brstrickland.com
I would love it if you subscribed to my blog and kept in touch. Feel free to contact me at: barb@brstrickland.com
www.goodreads.com
Amazon.com
Facebook
Twitter
Pintrest
Instagram

Books

Unexpected Obsession (The Unexpected Series Book 1)
eBook and Print copy
Emotions in Eruption (A poetic journey through life)
eBook and Print copy
Emotions in Evolution (The poetic journey continues)
eBook and Print copy

TBA

The Narrow Hallway (a psychological and paranormal thriller stand-alone)
Unexpected Passion (The Unexpected Series Book 2)
Unexpected Christmas Gathering (The Unexpected Series, Book 3)
Unexpected Desire (The Unexpected Series Book 4)
Unexpected Summer Heat (The Unexpected Series Book 5)
Unexpected Outcomes (The Unexpected Series, Book 6)
Green Mists (a science fiction stand-alone romance)
Memories of the Heart (memoirs with a twist)
Lance finds Home (a children's book)

About the author

I'm an Aussie with an Italian heritage. The warmth and beauty of both cultures has always inspired me, and I thought mixing it all together and adding a few other cultures in my books would be fun. I grew up in a multi-cultural environment with a dream to speak as many languages as possible, travel till there is no more to be seen, and own a dog and cat and have space for them both. I have a degree in teaching, three children and some amazing grandchildren and love reading, reading and more reading.

Unexpected Obsession (this novel is currently being updated-edit and should be available December 2018)
The Unexpected Series Book 1

Chapter 1

THE SCRAPE OF the chair on the cream tiles unnerved her. The noise was an intrusion reminding her, she was unwanted here. She sat down anyway. If Lia hadn't been internally shaking from fear, she thought, she might have laughed at the two people battling to deal with her audacity, and she might have felt a little embarrassed at her behaviour.
"What the devil are you doing here? You can't be serious!" Domenico was spitting enough fire to make a dragon proud. His height, the dark eyes intense and glaring, and the tight mouth were enough on their own to make her nervous. The quiet menace in his voice was an unwanted extra. Angelia looked searchingly at the man in front of her. The gangly sixteen-year old with the pretty-boy looks had disappeared. His place was taken by a very tall and well-built stranger. The dark close to black hair was just short of military precision. Domenico's face was close shaven. The man looked like he had stepped out of a Hollywood golden era, in his black suit (designer label of course), pristine white shirt, and bold red tie. Even the black leather shoes were immaculate.

Nothing here existed of the boy, the one her seven-year-old self, had worshipped. He had towered over her, a closed, aloof scowling giant to her smaller self. Somehow, she had gotten through the barriers to win his affection. Not once had she feared him. At almost twenty-eight years of age her height had caught up but not enough to stop her feeling just a little afraid of the man he had become. This time around those barriers were chillingly impregnable.

She swallowed and concentrated on the couple. They on the other hand, did not seem so different. Twenty years had only aged them. Gina looked so much like Papa that Lia felt a stab at her heart. Gina had been Papa's stepsister. Nonno had remarried after Nonna Maria died. Nonna Enza had a child, a scandal in the family because she hadn't been married and no-one knew who the father was. Papa had told Lia that Nonna Enza had been related in some fashion and hence he and Gina had looked so alike it had cemented a strong sibling relationship. Gina, Papa had told Lia, had always believed Antonio to be a surprise her parents had brought home just for her. He had been her baby, not just her little step-brother. Funny, Lia thought as an unpleasant trickle of cold slid along her spine, how one terrible moment in the past had shattered so many relationships, so many lives.

"Are you listening? What the hell are you doing here?"

"I rang first, remember?" She met his gaze bravely, aware that flinching would give him the upper hand.

"Domenico, you told her not to come? Why is she here?" Gina clutched at her heart. Unsteady in her gait, Gina leaned against the wall as she spoke. Domenico moved swiftly. He reached his mother before she lost her balance. He growled at Angelia. It made her feel sick inside. Someone else stood there watching, a thoughtful look on his face. Recognising her Uncle Lucio, Lia braced herself for another emotional outburst. Lucio remained quiet. His head tilted in surprise, but he still managed to rein in his expression enough to puzzle her. She remembered a different man, one of quick action, not this silent bystander who seemed out of place in his own home.

"You're my family. I don't need an invitation. I have every right to be here." She threw the letter she had written to them a scarce few months ago on the table. It had been returned unopened, unread just like all the other letters her father had sent to his sister over the years. "Since there is obviously something wrong with the Italian postal service, I thought I'd deliver the letter, my letter, to you in person. Funny thing though, it was marked return to sender from right here in Catania. Strange isn't it? Never mind. I have it here now. You know the letter I mean, the one about my father's accident. The one that told you he died." She released the bit of air that she had been holding in. The sound was loud in her ears. She looked away, focusing on the apartment; determined Domenico would not rattle her. It looked familiar, spotless from floor to ceiling, and the dining table was the same, a dark rich mahogany. Uncle Lucio had made it himself, and that little bit of knowledge from so long ago gave her confidence, despite the looming presence making her heart beat faster.

"Is this how people in Australia behave? They walk into someone's home, unannounced, and uninvited?" She turned away from staring at the older man, distracted by the younger one's harsh tone. She hid her shaking hands behind her back, glad he was a distance from her.

Over near the cream leather lounge where he had placed his mother, the aura he exuded was easier to handle. The lounge, another thing she remembered. Idly she mused that good pieces were pieces you kept. So why then had her aunt been so willing to throw away a lifetime of memories of the only family she had? Surely people mattered more than things?

"I told you on the phone we knew, wasn't that enough? Your father is dead..." Domenico stopped short as his mother let out an anguished moan. His face hardened further. "I'll say this in your language Angelia, in English so there is no misunderstanding. We don't need to know any more about him or you. Naturally we sympathise but that's as far as it goes. We aren't interested in any other letters and we aren't interested in you."

"Well, isn't that too fucking bad!" Lia muttered back, making sure he could see her mouth enunciating English words. If Domenico was fluent, and he was with that almost perfect pronunciation, then she was sure he would lip read her correctly. His mouth tightened, and she smiled, a little smug at his understanding. He was fucking with her brain. Speaking to her in English as if she was a stranger, making her feel like an outsider. *Not in this lifetime, dickhead.* "I thought my aunt," she replied, in Italian and with volume, enunciating each word carefully, "might need a sympathetic ear. After all, he was the only family she had left."

"Listen to me, little girl." Gina's snarl reverberated as pain in Lia's heart, the heart searching to find the aunt she remembered. Gina was still a pretty woman despite the lines of discord marring her forehead. Her uncoloured hair needed a trim but otherwise suited her. Some women looked good going grey and Gina was one of them. "I don't need or want you here. How I feel is my business, so get out. Go home!"

The pain at Gina's obvious lack of regard or affection changed to fear at the paleness of her aunt's face, at the veins now prominent in the forehead, shiny and slick with moisture, and at the obvious breathing difficulties. A panic attack, Lia thought. Domenico was whispering calming words, but his dark eyes were turned on Lia, fierce and narrowed. None of this was going to plan. What had she expected? In her peripheral vision she saw her uncle make a move towards Gina. He halted at the vicious look his son gave him. Lia swallowed and bit the inside of her cheek, willing herself to keep still. *God there was so much happening here!* The words pounded in Lia's head. If she moved, they would see her fear and she couldn't allow that.

The letters were supposed to explain. Over the years her Papa had written his sister about everything in their lives, good and bad. She had thought to convince her aunt to read them. She hadn't thought it through. Lia hadn't realised how fragile Gina was in body. Never a large woman, she was now a small frame of breakable bones. Lia bit down on her lip with despair at the thought that not even her brother's death could dent the bitterness and hatred emanating from Gina.

"You heard her! Get out!" Domenico's voice was a bombardment. His attention on her lip worse somehow. She stopped biting on it, perturbed by the sharp gaze.

"And you," Domenico barked in Italian without turning his head to his father, "go get her medication, or has this one dazzled you with her looks the way her slut of a mother did."

His continued focus on her mouth was uncomfortable. His satisfaction at this was on his face but he had miscalculated with his words. Even if he had reason to say what he did, where Marissa was concerned, it was cruel, an unnecessary taunt. It touched a raw nerve and gave purpose and strength back to Lia.

"I'm staying even if I have to sleep on the floor." Lia stood up and walked over to where she had placed her bags. She picked up her back pack from where it rested on the ground, pulled out a plastic bag and turned to face her aunt. "This has every letter my father wrote. I am not leaving until I see you read, each, and every one of them. He loved you. He needed you, not your punishment. I know your reasons were good ones. They belong in the past. It may be too late for him; it's not too late for me to do this for him. You are going to read every word and then I'll go. Mark my words, you will read them. He deserves to be remembered." Lia tilted her head, letting her expression show her determination.

"Who do you think you're dealing with?" Domenico was suddenly standing in front of her. His eyes had darkened to a black abyss holding hers, prisoner. The intimidating look, the same one he had given her on opening the door strengthened her resolve. Lia held her ground, staring straight into the void. No doubt this same scenario would be repeated. She shrugged as if she hadn't a care in the world, turning away. The relief to be away from that unyielding stare nearly buckled her knees. "You're just a rude, arrogant little bitch!" His voice was a low hiss behind her, his tone menacing, the English words cold.

"It's obvious we are related then," she replied in Italian. "Although I would think arsehole suits you much better. It's more masculine." She turned and held that last word just long enough to let him know she wholeheartedly doubted the latter. Smiling inwardly, she reflected his tirade was quite mild compared to the words he might have used in his own language. That was the beauty of the Italian language, she thought, letting herself be distanced from the scene in front of her for a moment, to recoup. Swearing and name-calling were extremely creative.

His reply was a supercilious sneer, annoying Lia further. She didn't censor what came next. "Perhaps, a rude arrogant bastard is more apt? Bastard, being the operative word, I'd imagine." Her words were beneath her. The gasp from her aunt testified to just how much that was true. She deserved the terrifying anger she glimpsed in Domenico before his face smoothed over.

His body was still coiled tight. Lia felt his physical battle to relax his shoulders before giving her a dismissive look. Her own body remained tense with shame. Her retort had been nasty. This wasn't her way. She wanted to erase her words but didn't know how; backing down was not an option. Fortunately, she had an unexpected reprieve from the one other person who might also have taken offence at her words.

"Leave her alone. This is my house and I say she can stay."

"Well, of course old man, you would come to her rescue. You fucked her mother in this very home, so what now? The daughter?"

Lia cringed at the crude, spiteful way Domenico had chosen to re-direct his anger at her. Lucio stood resolute, not even a blink. Lia found it painful to watch, especially since her aunt seemed unmoved by this interchange. The skin of her face though was paler, almost grey. Not the steely hue of her thick hair, but a pasty looking imitation.

"Take your mother to her room. She needs her pills and to lie down. Keep your opinions to yourself. I repeat – this is my house." His voice was quiet, yet it had an underlying strength. Not surprisingly, Domenico did as he was asked. Lia let go of the breath she was holding. Her chest no longer restricted, she turned her eyes to Lucio.

"Thank you! I'm so sorry."

"This is a very complicated household. My son took it easy on you. Next time he won't be as pleasant." She made a rude sound and he laughed. "Believe me, he let you off lightly. He is very possessive and very protective where his mother is concerned, and he was worried about her. Me, he doesn't care too much for."

Despite the silver flecks in his hair, Lucio was still an exceptionally handsome man. The bone structure heralded antiquity. A strong jaw line and an almost perfectly, oval shaped face was reminiscent of statues of Roman gods. He was taller, too, than many Italian men, about half a head under six feet, and had an air of confidence, at least when his son's piercing gaze wasn't aimed at him. His son, Lia suspected, never lost that arrogant tilt of eyebrows. Yes. Lucio was very good-looking. So was his son. Even more so, because whilst Domenico had that same facial structure, he also had a look of Gina in the bone structure around his eyes, eyes dark like the most decadent chocolate, with long lashes most women would envy. Her father had the same eyes and so did she. Without them she would have been a clone of Marissa, her mother.

"You're different to what I expected." Lia narrowed her gaze to focus on Lucio. The cocky self-assuredness she remembered was missing. Even as a child she had noted, his confidence in his appeal as a male, in his ability to charm.

"More charming?"

She couldn't help indulging his use of that word with a small laugh. He shrugged self-deprecatingly. Lia could see sadness in those eyes.

"Age softens and changes things for some. Your aunt, my wife, is a hard woman. She lost a child and did considerable damage to her leg and we both know the how and why of it, don't we?" He waited for Lia to acknowledge his words. At her nod he continued. "I think it's too late for her to change her feelings and her ways. I'm telling you so you won't be disappointed even..."

Lia waited for him to continue, realising he was mellower, more approachable as if the edge had been rubbed right off him. Back then his good looks and surety had scared her a little. "Even...?"

"Even as I am hoping you succeed. Domenico will fight you being here. Ignore him. You are welcome to stay as long, as you want. I meant what I said. This is my house."

"Thank you."

"You'll be sharing a bathroom with Domenico."

Lucio's raised eyebrows made her smile. "Is he still a clean freak?"

"You're still that bright little girl, aren't you?" Lucio laughed quietly in reply. "You have a good memory, and yes he is. Everything must have a place, usually where he puts it. Don't leave a wet sink. There are paper towels to wipe the basin down. Can you cope?"

"You're enjoying this, aren't you?" She smiled wryly, pleased to see a twinkle in his eyes wiping some of the sadness away.

"It might be just what this family needs," he replied. The twinkle was replaced with a more sombre look. "Lia, Domenico is harsh and lives by rules, usually his, but he is a good person. Too strong, far too precise in expectations, yet for all that, he has never shirked family responsibility, even with me. Give him time. Now, do you want a coffee?"

She nodded again, understanding his need to shift the conversation.

"Uncle Lucio, will she be alright? She didn't look too good."

"She gets emotional and needs medication for her heart. Your aunt...your aunt is stronger than she thinks. She didn't believe you would come. Gina hates confrontations, and to be honest she has hung on to her bitterness for so long she doesn't know anything else. Seeing you is...conflicting. She loved you so much. We all did."

He turned away, heading for the kitchen. Lia frowned. Despite all she knew of the past, she found this Lucio likeable.

"Are you sure about this?"

Halting, he turned at her question. "You look shattered! Why don't you settle into your room? Stop thinking, there's plenty of time for that."

His words made her feel safe and strangely wanted. Lia walked back to her bags, picked them up and carried them to the room with a lighter heart. She would need sheets, but Lucio was already there, handing her towels and linen before disappearing. He moved gracefully, a trait she had noticed in Domenico who had prowled the room like a cat. Lia sat on the bed, wondering again what she had got herself into, because the reality was not just this room. It comprised dinner, lunch, breakfast, using the bathroom, sleeping and doing all this in a house where she wasn't wanted.

Lucio came back with coffee. He had also thoughtfully prepared a tray containing biscuits, cheese and olives. He was quiet, unobtrusive as he put the things he carried on the small bedside table. The sadness was back in his eyes.

"I've brought you a spare set of keys." Pausing he held her eyes. "They will fight you. Just ignore them and treat this as your home. Eat when we eat. Gina will feed you. It is her way and it might provide an avenue for discussion, or not." He shrugged, looking self-conscious at Lia's intent stare. "She cooks for me, washes and irons my clothes despite the fact we haven't shared much else for twenty years, and she will do the same for you and hate you just as much. She's like that."

"Why? Why are you really allowing this?

"I owe Antonio. He was a good man, one of the best. He was my friend not just my brother-in-law. The past is a heavy burden at this age. Maybe you are the key to change. I am so tired of the cold. Today for the first time I felt a little warmth. You have brought the sun."

"Solare," she whispered at his retreating back. That had been his word for her back then, teasing her that she was sunshine. She sat for a long time after he left. Dinner that evening was not pleasant, but she stayed, refusing to be baited by either mother or son.

Chapter 2

GINA WOULD play old records on an antiquated record player as she did the housework, and sometimes she would sing. Her voice was soft and sweet and unexpected from someone who had seemingly forgotten to smile. The first morning Lia sang along was the first time she felt Gina really saw her and not her mother, not Marissa. It wasn't hard to feel emotion and put it into the singing, after a fortnight of being ignored except in the evenings when Lucio returned from work. The ignoring did have its merits though. Shivering, even now a week later, she recalled the encounter with Domenico. It had almost sent her running home.

"Don't you know to knock?"

"This is my home, not yours, remember?"

"What do you want?"

"To give you a friendly word of warning, my dear sweet little cousin."

"Step-cousin more like it, and the little bit of blood we share is about two generations removed, thank you very much. Not that it makes a difference. Either way I'm pretty sure, your family welcome would still be underwhelming." Lia had barely restrained the smirk. Her fear of starting something held her in check and only for her aunt's sake.

"I'm watching you. I'm not my father to be swayed by looks."

His gaze had moved insolently from the pale pink polished toe nails and bare feet and slowly up, stopping only when he reached her mouth. She had read too many books to let her teeth bite down on her bottom lip. The temptation was strong; it was an instinctive action. He made her uneasy, and not because he made her feel unwelcome. She wasn't sure she needed or wanted to know the reason. It was enough she understood it was his intention to make her uncomfortable. His striking presence was unsettling. Looks and personality, however, could be so at odds. She remained silent but didn't look away.

"My mother has been through too much in her life. Hurt her in any fashion and I'll make you sorry in ways you can't possibly imagine. I won't let a stronza like you contaminate the air around her."

"So, you can use the Italian language when it suits you. You're the only one doing the hurting from where I sit. I don't want to hurt anyone."

"Forgive my foolish assumption. It couldn't be because your behaviour in forcing yourself on us suggests no morals or manners."

"Thanks for the little chat. I think the only stronzo here is you. It's long overdue for you to put a sock in it. I've been trying to be polite, avoid arguments, and show you I do have manners!"

His jaw tightened in disdainful and dismissive amusement. "A sock? Is this some clever Australianism you are imparting on my poor, ignorant brain?"

His tone was polite and yet it flowed with arrogance. How did he manage that? How did he manage to make her feel stupid? "Yes, I said sock. To be exact I said put a sock in it. So, it seems you are not familiar with this particular expression. I'm surprised, as I have been quite impressed at your command of English. I can only surmise you had an excellent teacher."

Domenico just lifted the one eyebrow and waited; complete distaste for her all too evident.

"How can I explain?" Lia was close to saturation point. If he wasn't making nasty comments, he acted as if she didn't exist and spoke around her. Domenico presumed and accused, and continually taunted, despite her best efforts to be friendly, to be nice and to find her way back to the warmth and affection that had existed in the past. She suspected he knew that and took pleasure in the opposite. Perhaps what she wanted was unrealistic in these early days. Right now, though, her anger was too far gone to listen to reason.

She turned in her chair and used the wheels to push away from the desk until she was closer to him. "I said, put a sock in it, right here." Lia stretched over as she spoke and grabbed his crotch and twisted. "A sock in here will ensure that everyone understands how big a dick you actually are, not have, but are. Although I need to stress, if your dick is as pathetic as your behaviour, then it too, might be an issue, a small one but an issue."

The look on his face was priceless; her enjoyment short-lived. Domenico grabbed her wrist, forcing her hand to envelop him, a 'him', or 'it' that was a little bigger and harder than she needed to know. It throbbed. She squirmed. A feeling she couldn't even think about caused her hand to flicker against him and he, it, the thing she couldn't give a name to, jerked against her fingers. For a split second she pushed against him slowly, curiously fascinated by the way it seemed to shape itself to her hand, and the way it felt, hard and soft at the same time. Common sense and reality reared, snapping her to attention. Lia tried to pull away.

"You think you are so smart! You foolish little girl! You have no idea what you're up against. Don't ever touch me again unless you're invited, or you will get so much more than you bargained for." Domenico gave her a smug look as the colour rose from her neck to the roots of her hair.

She heard herself make a small clicking sound as she struggled to prevent the grimace her face was pursuing as she felt the embarrassing warmth pervade her cheeks. Lia tried harder to tug her hand away. He just pressed it tighter against his body. She couldn't look at him. "You already seem to have the more. Feels good, doesn't it? Or at least it does to me. I guess my dick doesn't discriminate as well as I do."

Her anger spiked. Lia squeezed and twisted hard. She wanted to hurt. Lia heard the hitch in Domenico's breathing as he tightened his grip on her wrist so cruelly she had to open her hand. He was now hurting her. But, it was worth it. He had expected her to fight him but not attack again and he hadn't been ready. She looked up in satisfaction only to have that look die under the blaze of heat in his eyes.

"Well, well, well, it seems to me you have quite a bit of your mother in you, don't you? Like playing with dicks, do we?"

"I don't know about playing, but in your case 'dick' is the point I was trying to make." She tried to pull away. He exerted even more pressure to keep her hand in place.

"What a clever play on words. Don't look so surprised. I did have very good teachers. Good enough to know you need to widen your vocabulary. You do seem to enjoy the word 'dick'. I prefer cock myself."

The flame of heat in his eyes contrasted sharply with the coldness in his voice. Keeping her hand in his grasp he moved it to brush the solid length in a sweeping motion. His use of the word cock had shocked her. The inappropriateness was distracting, and it gave him control. Instinctively her fingers spread to cover him. In reaction his cock jerked against her hand again. The feeling it stirred created an odd connection to the more intimate parts of her body.

Lia felt sick. She glared at the face sculpted in stone. Domenico let her go. She wiped her hand ruthlessly on her jeans. The stone face cracked a little with a small smug laugh before it closed off again with an indifference that made her want to hit him. Something in his gaze though, made her wary. Lia was smart enough to recognise she was in over her head.

"That was disgusting, you are disgusting!" she muttered, completely flustered and furious and not at all able to *understand a situation he had turned around so easily to his advantage. How had he gained the upper hand?*

"Really? I fucking loved it. Want me to return the favour? It might add a whole new dimension to our relationship."

"What a total arsehole you are!"

"Why? Because I won 'this round'? I always win. If you don't like it, leave." Nico walked out, leaving her shaken and puzzled, and dismayed at the fact that she had referred to him as Nico even if it occurred in her mind. Why that small fact bothered her the most, considering the entire situation, was far too complex to contemplate.

The sound of her aunt's voice brought her back to the present.

"Back from the land of the fairies, are we? So, did he teach you the songs?"

Words, and not just a look or semi-growl, were a decided improvement despite the tone. Lia schooled her features to hide her excitement. She looked up from her computer where she sat every morning.

"Yes. Or sometimes it would be Mama, especially when she was sick. It helped her pass the time."

"Always the old songs, he liked the old songs, especially this one. Ha! *Calabria Mia* of all things!" Gina huffed, ignoring any mention of Lia's mother.

Lia had hoped her willingness to help around the house and with the cooking had softened Gina a little, but her aunt was not an easy person to get through to. "It's what it represented. Sicily, Calabria, in the end they all were Italians who'd left their homes, left their families. They were lonely for those things. Please read his letters," Lia asked, as she did every day, not ashamed of the plea in her voice.

"So determined!" Gina huffed again and turned away.

"Yes. You owe it to your brother."

"I don't owe anybody anything. I did nothing, it was done to me, remember? I am sure you know the story, you seem to know everything." She had her back to Lia. She went quiet and then turned slowly to glance slyly at Lia. "Tell me, little girl, will you tell me about the nightmares if I do read one?"

"Why?" It took all of Lia's self-control not to react to the sudden change in conversation.

"I'm curious about you. I don't remember you as such a rude child and I wondered maybe if guilt was manifesting itself. It can't be easy to be where you are; so obviously unwanted."

Lia shut down her computer and tried hard not to let the hurt show. So, what if she wasn't the little girl adored by her aunt? There were worse things in life. Things like losing both parents. Lia stood and walked slowly forward stopping directly in front of Gina.

"You're so determined to be the wicked, hateful witch, aren't you? Here's your chance to gloat. It's true. It's all about guilt. Too bad it's not quite the way you might imagine." Lia lifted her arms to the back of her dress, unzipped it and slowly turned her body so Gina had a good view of her back. She eased the dress aside so that Gina could follow the unsightly-looking pink line around to the front of her body. She heard Gina's surprised indrawn breath and cringed a little. Lia didn't want pity. Then again, pity was an honest emotion, and Lia wasn't too proud to take whatever she could get.

"You were there? In the car? No one told us."

"Does it matter? It doesn't make my father less dead, does it, or me, any less guilty for surviving." A gasp was followed by a tangible silence. Lia used the opportunity to pull the blue fabric back up. She almost winced when soft hands took over sliding the zip.

"How?"

Lia turned and stared at her aunt, debating the wisdom of revealing so much. The details weren't pleasant. Did Gina need the reality of the accident? Would it make her more amiable, more likely to remember the little brother she once adored? What if Lia could reach both the loving aunt and her father's sister? Lia had to try, so she hoped her smile didn't reflect the bitterness she felt. "What do you want to know?"

***

A long time, later Lia stood, left the kitchen and came back to the table to place the first letter down in front of the tear-stained face of an old woman. Lia found the letter untouched when she returned an hour later from her room. Her aunt wasn't in the apartment; Lia hadn't heard her leave. She sat down and stared at the envelope as if waiting for an answer. *There was always tomorrow and the next day. It's not like I have to get back for work. Most of it is online.* Lia was restless. It wouldn't help her win this war of nerves. If she was to be honest, she was very disappointed in everything about this trip, at least where her family were concerned.

At the beginning she had been unsure about coming. Lia had thought Papa was trying to force things. Slowly Lia had come around. Why have families if you let them fall apart? Why then did people bother having children? Families were important; they sustained you. Sometimes things happened; it was the nature of people. Lia understood things could bring pain, but families forgave. Living in bitterness wasn't the answer. Where was the Gina she remembered, the affectionate sister, the loving aunt who had wanted a little girl just like Angelia? That woman had demonstrated an amazing capacity to feel.

Lia sighed. Her aunt was right. The damage had been done to Gina, and despite her own brother's death Gina didn't know how to let go of that. Lia wanted the affection back. She needed it. Papa had been right to want this for her. Even with all the angst, a companionship had developed between them. Gina could deny it till she was blue in the face, but Lia felt it growing. She wanted to stay. She wanted a little of that first time here so many years ago, and she wanted her superhero. She laughed at herself. *Domenico was not going to be an easy conquest.*

Things were hard enough with her aunt. Lia's shoulders shrugged dismissively. *Time to be more positive.* The boy had been so annoyed with her persistence in following him around. And then, Domenico had given in. All it had taken was for the seven-year-old Lia to put her hand in his to cross the road. He had raised those dark brows and she had smiled, not at all rebuffed by his scowl. "*Have it your way then.*" She had smiled again at his answer. He proceeded to indulge her from that day despite the teasing of his friends. That boy was still there surely even if buried in the layers of the man. Lia had patience, and she reminded herself she was a strategic planner.

Her aunt was the key to harmony. Maybe another way was possible to break down the barriers between them, a simpler way that might also ease the boredom of the wait. Lia needed to do some shopping for the project spinning around in her head.

***

The pattern she had chosen was simple but interesting, to encourage interaction. Pinning the squares together to make rows was a slow procedure, as the seams had to be exact. It had the desired outcome. Too strong-willed to ask questions, by the end of the week Gina had stopped resisting the lure of brightly coloured fabric and joined Lia at the table, quietly observing, never uttering a word and never picking up the letter that waited there every day. The battle of wills was a gentle lull, spoiled only when Domenico came home for lunch. *If looks could kill* Lia would have shrivelled up weeks ago.

This morning was different. Last night Gina had come in and soothed her when she had dreamt of the accident, and then waited until Lia had fallen asleep again. Now, Gina had actually picked up the pieces of material to touch them, the dressmaker in her unable to stop the need. When Gina had replaced the pieces on the table, Lia swallowed, almost afraid to breathe, as the rustle of paper was heard. She continued sewing and didn't look up once until her aunt put the letter down and silently shuffled away.

Lia picked it up and took it to her room and placed it in the plastic bag with the others. She took another one out before returning the bag to the dresser drawer. Neither woman had spoken about the previous night, yet something had changed. Tomorrow, the second letter would be on the table waiting for Gina, just as the next time the memories woke Lia, a hand would be there to chase away the darkness. *I won't make more of this than it is*, Lia kept telling herself.

***

Gina had read a letter a day now for over a week. She had also become quite vocal about the quilt Lia was creating. No other more normal conversation occurred yet the feeling of companionship continued to flourish. This morning they had baked. Later they had enjoyed the cake with coffee before setting up the sewing machine. When the phone rang, and Gina pointedly looked at Lia, she struggled not to roll her eyes at her aunt. Domenico always rang at this time.

"Pronto"

"Where's my mother?" The voice was curt, dismissive and distinctly annoyed. Lia thought of it as his trifecta tone, three winning ways to piss off Lia. She wondered what he would think of that little piece of Australianism. *There go my good intentions.* Gina would get her performance.

"Well hello to you too and thanks for asking, and yes I am well. What can I do for you?" Any conversation they had was always conducted in English. He was determined to make her feel distanced from the family, from the whole country. Lia found it amusing.

"Leave Italy but put my mother on the phone first."

Lia held the phone towards Gina.

"Tell him I'm busy and he can talk to you." Lia bit the inside of her cheek at her aunt's little game.

"She can't talk right now. Can I take a message?" Lia smiled, knowing exactly how irate he'd be at Lia's saccharine sweet tone, and his mother's behaviour. Lia and Nico both knew Gina received some sort of perverse pleasure from their confrontations even if conducted in a foreign language. Neither one though was prepared to back off. The result as usual, was an unpleasant conversation with Domenico.

"I'll tell her," Lia said very politely. "Please do enjoy the rest of your day."

"Why, have you packed your bags?"

"Go fuck yourself."

"Such beautiful manners. You know, as a matter of fact, I was just about to follow that suggestion, but not on my own."

"You're a pig." With those words she slammed the phone down. She didn't miss the glimpse of humour on the normally dour face before her aunt swiftly looked away. "He's not coming home for lunch and won't be home tonight either."

"Probably Francesca again!" Gina puffed her displeasure.

It hadn't taken Lia long to learn Francesca was not liked. Having met her briefly, Lia understood perfectly. Francesca was a beautiful, egotistical bitch.

"Intelligent enough when she can get past herself. Too bad that doesn't happen often. My Nico should know better, even if her father is an important man..." Gina stopped, Lia surmised, on realising she was actually making conversation.

"They deserve each other. They're both arrogant arseholes!" Lia looked up suddenly, realising she spoken out loud. The pleasant atmosphere had just evaporated. Lia could see it reflected in the distortion of features on Gina's face.

"Because I read the letters you think you have rights now, to criticise my son and his choice of partner?"

"No, I'm sorry. I didn't mean to say anything."

"Yes! You did! You don't like my son. I'll admit he isn't very nice to you. Coming here with an agenda negated winning a popularity contest, especially since no thought was given to whom you may hurt or impose on, correct?" Gina didn't wait for a reply. "He may be difficult at times. Don't pull that face. He is my son so you, you need to keep your mouth shut. I don't care what he says to you or about you, but I do care what you say *about* him. Not to him but about him, so be very careful, Angelia, very careful."

"That isn't fair Aunt Gina. He is so..."

"Don't!"

"But..."

"I said, don't! Now let me finish reading and then another coffee and you can tell me more about Sydney."

Lia knew she would lose the little ground she had gained if she protested. She continued working in silence while her aunt went back to the letter. *There was always tomorrow. Si, domani!* Lia sighed. She seemed to be repeating the tomorrow phrase constantly, almost as often as she sighed these days. Her determination was faltering. Domenico had that effect. She kept looking for the hero of years ago and instead kept slamming up against the sharp, hard planes of a man who left the bathroom spotless and smelling expensive, exclusive and so excluding where she was concerned.

She understood he upset her equilibrium with his refusal to accept her back into the family fold. Their constant bickering shrouded something cavernous. At times an insidious element celebrated his rejection. Lia thought of it as an unexpected and complicated puzzle piece. She kept her eyes on the fabric in her hands.

***

"Fuck!" Domenico slammed the phone down on his desk in his office on the other side of the city. Something about her grated in a way he couldn't ignore. She had just walked in like she owned the place, stirring up emotions best forgotten. As if, he thought, his mother hadn't been hurt enough already with the events of the past, they now had a living reminder. In every movement, every look, the way she held her head he saw Marissa come to life, except for the eyes. Marissa's had been a sea green and her hair a touch lighter. Even so, the resemblance was uncanny and all of it pissed him off.

However, Lia's mouth annoyed him the most. The things she came out with, the language despite the innocence of that perfect face. Those little comments about his being a mamma's boy because he still lived at home were wearing thin. Lia pronounced it *mama*, an Australian idiosyncrasy that further grated on his nerves. Although he had to admit, he did incite her at every opportunity; a perverse entertainment. Domenico enjoyed making her miserable, especially since he couldn't forget the way she had stood up to him that day. A part of him had applauded her recklessness. At the same time, he wanted to squash her like a fly. *She had actually touched his dick!* He had never felt such anger or such a heated response. He still didn't know how he managed to stay in control of both his temper and his body. Her defiance had aroused him, had unleashed a heat he had not thought possible. It stilled burned. *That one moment when she had leaned into his rigid cock, her hand shaping...fuck her.* Why couldn't she take the hints and go back to Australia? He gave them out often enough.

Of course, the old man rushed in to defend her at every opportunity. He was eating the attention up. Who knew what went on in his mind, fawning all over her and her sweet little ways? Why was his mother being so quiet about it all? After the initial outbursts she hadn't said much at all.

He adored his mother. She'd always made him feel safe, and powerful. Not once had she complained when he needed his room a certain way, his things arranged in a certain order.

"Mamma, they have to go back exactly like this."

His father on the other hand...Nico knew the old man resented finding himself having to marry Gina. He could accept those feelings. They had certain logic. Being made to take on a wife and child for propriety couldn't have been easy. That Lucio couldn't accept Domenico's inability to fit the image in Lucio's mind of what a *son* should be was unforgivable. Now Lia had brought the whole situation to the forefront again, just by existing. His whole routine at home was thrown out.

"I don't get it." He paced around the room as he spoke and then came back to stop directly in front of his mother. "Has she become your little pet?"

"Domenico, Nico, that's not exactly a kind way to refer to the girl," she replied, not hiding her amusement at his rant.

"Well, now you're reading the letters, letting her play with your sewing machine and having cosy little meetings at the kitchen table. What the hell Ma?"

"She entertains me. She is such a determined little thing and she has some right on her side."

"What's the matter Ma? And don't shake that head at me!"

"She makes me feel lonely and confused but..."

"That's it, she has to go."

"No, you don't understand. What I mean is, she is making me see how narrow my life is and..."

"I'm not enough? Do I make it too much with my ways?"

"Nico, I enjoy doing things for you. You know that."

"No, I ask too much. I demand too much! The bitch is right. I should have my own place."

"Nico, stop! I'll admit you can be challenging," she had said with that wide smile and her eyes radiating love and warmth. "It's hard to explain, but she fills a void. In some ways she isn't so different to you, you know. She likes *things clean and tidy, and she helps me willingly. I like it...I..."*

"It's an act, this being so helpful. Come on, Ma. She has an agenda, a twisted one that justifies forcing herself on us."

"No, it's her. Can you let me talk?" He had nodded, if unwillingly and she had continued. "She is a sharer, of her heart and maybe a little of her soul, she has...I can't explain but she brings the sun. Solare, you father would say when she was little. Don't pout, my son. It's not like we have to admit any of this to her."

"No, she looks too much like Marissa not to have some of her nature. I don't want her here, and if she hurts you in any way...."

"You and I, Nico, have never needed anybody else. Maybe that's not right. We do need others. Leave her alone. I'm not asking you to be nice to her."

"I love you Mamma, so whatever makes you happy. You need to know I don't like it. I don't like her!"

"You did once."

"She was a child then, sweet, not this bitch with letter issues."

"Domenico, he was my brother. He was my family. Leave her alone, for me."

"Fuck!" he growled back in the present. He turned to face the woman in his office.

"Did you lock the door after Ivana left? Good girl," he said, tracing a finger from her cheek to the full red lips when she nodded. He inserted his finger and she was quick to suck on it. His cock jerked in response. "And what else did you do?" In reply Francesca dangled a black lace thong. He took it and tossed it to the floor. Tangling his hands in the back of her long thick hair, he pushed her face down towards his desk. Still holding her hair, he halted so she was just hovering, a breath away from the solid timber. "Do you see all my files, my pens, how nicely they are laid out?" He pulled on her hair and she nodded. "Good, now remember no matter what I don't want any disruption to my desk. I have work to do later."

With those words he pushed her head down so her forehead was on the surface of the desk. He placed her hands flat above her head over the files he was working on. "Now don't move" he ordered. He hitched up her skirt, shoving his knee between her legs, pushing her thighs apart without any finesse. She whimpered, thrusting her behind higher. Presumptuous bitch, he thought, tugging her hair cruelly. Indulging her wasn't a hardship on the odd occasion it suited him.

Today, foreplay wasn't going to happen. She wouldn't even murmur in protest, just as she never murmured when he refused to kiss her. Francesca never knew when and what he would decide to do; it kept her eager. He initiated. She followed. He tugged her hair harder. She whimpered again, widening her stance and lifting the smooth tanned skin in a way that made it only too obvious what she wanted, what she always wanted. Her bottom was so tight. Her slit glistened. He pushed her dress up higher. She groaned, and he grinned to himself.

"Do you want my cock here?" he said, thrusting two fingers into her slickness. She moaned but shook her head. He taunted her some more before unzipping his pants. Nico let her go to sheath himself, impatient to be done. He thrust his fingers back inside her and then used the moisture on his fingers around the opening of her anus. Her whole body trembled, and his cock leaped, responding to her excitement. One long finger was replaced by two. She panted, she moaned. She whimpered like a baby. He gave her more. He felt her muscles coiling in anticipation and reached for the little bottle on his desk. Generous with the lubrication didn't mean he gave her warning. Instead he grabbed her hips and thrust deeply. Francesca arched and cried out in pain, the kind of pain she loved.

"Yes, yes. More. Give me more."

"Do you want me to stop?" he asked harshly, his voice roughened by desire. "Answer me."

"God no," she screeched, shoving against him, impatient as always.

"Then don't tell me how I should fuck you." He pulled out and walked around to the front of the desk. She stayed perfectly still under his glare, watching as he moved his hand over his long, hard length. She salivated, licked her lips but remained quiet. He waited, staring and stroking continuously. She didn't make a sound. He walked back behind her and slid into cock heaven. A low groan escaped him at the fit. She was so tight, so desperate to set the pace. Francesca wanted that edgy pleasure badly. Nico smiled to himself. He hadn't intended to get into a serious relationship with her. Surprisingly, they suited each other well.

Francesca's pride or ego kept her faithful. She might like her sex specific and rough, but she wasn't a bed hopper. She felt herself above that. Francesca was a snob whose need to protect her reputation was at odds with her greedy, sexual and often perverse personality. If she wanted to look down on others, he didn't care. He cared that she was fastidious. In public, she used that cultured voice and well-dressed body to advantage. Her intelligence and her ability to act as a hostess were above par. It amused him to know her father was grooming her to take over the family business in the sincere belief his daughter only shit, gold nuggets. Francesca ensured her father kept thinking that way. Her sense of superiority wouldn't allow anything less.

The slap of his balls against her flesh was both delicious and painful. It brought him back to the current situation. Nico had work waiting for his attention. He needed to speed things up. Nico reached for her breast, pulling on the piercing so that she bucked against him. She screamed. Her breathing, wild and ragged, egged him on so he allowed it. He relished his control of her orgasms. Increasing his thrusts to pounding, he used his fingers to mimic his actions in her weeping slit. Nico knew just what she liked. She screamed again, and he let go. *Fuck, it felt good.*

He wasted no time pulling out of her, removed the condom, tied it up and put it into one of the small bags he kept for that purpose. He watched her, noting the smile on her face as she put on her panties. Francesca wasn't at all bothered by the coldness of his withdrawal. It excited her. She saw it as an appetiser for next time. As much as was possible they were happy together in a neat little package. Functioning for him depended on a controlled environment.

He walked to the bathroom and washed his hands, smelling his fingers to ensure no remnant remained of Francesca's essence. He washed them again and looked up in the mirror as he rinsed. *That mouth, that delicious annoying mouth with those full lips that pouted so delightfully at his jibes*, he said to his image in the oval mirror, *was going to get her into so much trouble. She had far too much to say for herself.* He shook himself in annoyance as he realised exactly who he was thinking about. It wasn't Francesca.

Chapter 3

"**Is this what** you bought at the markets? It's just one colour."
"I want it to contrast against the pattern. Can I use the sewing machine again?" Lia never knew if she should say more when Gina instigated these moments of not quite conversation. She had finally decided on keeping replies short and sweet. Gina gave a nod and went back to the letter. This was the letter Papa had sent three months into Mama's remission. Lia knew every word off by heart. *I pray every night that she is really finished with all the pain,* he had written. Her parents had been reconciled at this point, and Lia wasn't sure she could cope if Gina made any cutting comments.

Although lately she had seen a little of the woman she remembered, the thawing process in the cold war between them was slow. Ice was melting though. What surprised Lia was the fact that even if she had begun this process of wanting a truce for her father's sake, she now wanted it for herself. She was so caught up in her musings that she almost missed the moment Gina spoke.

"She suffered a great deal, didn't she?"

Lia nodded and picked up the material in her lap blindly. Her insides ached. Bile rose in her mouth. She forced it down, concentrating fiercely to remain silent and still.

"They loved each other?" This was one of those moments again. Moments Lia wasn't sure she should interrupt by speaking. Gina sounded as if she cared. Her voice was less stilted somehow, less harsh, almost kind.

"Yes," Lia finally whispered. "She told me near the end, that last year of her life was the happiest she had ever been."

"This is difficult for you, isn't it, despite the bravado you insist on whipping me with?" When Angelia didn't reply, her aunt continued. "You know everything, don't you, all the dirty bits and pieces of that awful day?" Gina sighed, a sad sound. "You ask for a lot being here, do you realise that? What is it you want? Because it's not just about these letters, not like in the beginning. And you and Lucio, such an inordinate amount of time spent talking so cosily, what is all that?"

"I like him. I want to bury the past and so does he. I think you know that. I want a family. They, my mother, my father and Lucio, paid a huge price for what they did..."

"And I didn't?"

"Aunt Gina, I know you did. It was terrible, but it's been twenty years. Lucio is still here. I know he's done some stupid things over the years, but you shut him out completely, turned his son against him, and yet he is still here."

"He talks too much."

"Aunt Gina! Please. He doesn't tell me these things. I'm not blind, I see the way things are. My mother paid; the things she faced with her illness you couldn't imagine.

Papa paid, he lost her; he lost you. Can this all stop before more people are dead without closure?"

Gina got up and left the room, but not before Lia had seen tears. Bitterness, loss and anger, all three had glided across that pale visage, and yet the real Gina had been there too, the old Gina. Despite the severity of unhappiness etched on that forehead, today something else had broken free. Lia wondered how people could keep feelings so bottled up inside, letting them twist their lives for so long. Her aunt needed time to think. Hell, *she* needed to think. What exactly was she here to accomplish? Gina was right. Much more was involved and all of it painfully frustrating.

"Lia?"

"Uncle Lucio, I didn't hear you come in."

"I didn't want to interrupt. You are so determined, like my son. When you want something, you don't let anything get in the way." Lia winced, and Lucio broke in quickly. "No, I didn't mean that in a bad way. I have watched you; you are kind, gentle, patient and you love her. I can see it. You even tolerate my son while he goes out of his way to make life so difficult." He sighed, weighing his words, understanding she was wary, and rightfully so. "I wanted to tell you…"

"Please don't say you're sorry. I am so sick of sorry. I just want to forget, to move on."

"I know that. I wanted to, not explain maybe but…" He sighed again. "I know you have details, memories perhaps and it was wrong, what we did. I don't want forgiveness. I do want you to understand."

He stopped talking and she could see he was searching for words. Out of the corner of her eye Lia noted Gina coming back down the hallway. "Uncle Lucio, stop, it doesn't matter." Lia was afraid Lucio might say something to ruin the precarious relationship she and her aunt seemed to be building. Gina's expression and the finger pressed to her aunt's lip silenced her.

"You told Gina we should have closure. You're right. Your mother and I, we never had closure. Closure is important. Gina's pregnancy took priority and so the passion we had for each other wasn't resolved. Now, I know it wouldn't have lasted. Then, your mother and I weren't given the option to find out. It became the ultimate fantasy of *what ifs*. I know it doesn't excuse what Marissa and I did. That summer we met again we were selfish. After living with a fantasy for so long, we couldn't resist finding out if it had a basis. We, your mother and I, selfishly but honestly too, believed we had to find out if it meant something. We were wrong, and in the process of finding out, we destroyed a family." The sound of his sigh was sad, a tiny, pitiful expulsion of breath. "I like it, you being here. I am so tired of all this drama. I want to turn it off like we do the television. But mostly, I don't want you to hate me."

"God," she said, her voice quivery despite a great effort to maintain neutrality. Lia couldn't dismiss the woman listening, as the man in front of her, bared his soul. "I forced my way into your home and you helped me. I don't hate you. I hate what you did that day. I understand the reasoning if not the deed. Mama explained the same thing to me. We might not be able to forget the past but maybe we can…"

"Maybe we can accept that people can change?"

Longing was there in his face and in his voice. Lia couldn't reply; she didn't know how.

"The trouble is: some us find it harder to believe people can learn from their mistakes. Your mother learned, and your father forgave her. I want the same thing. Convincing Gina and Domenico…"

"You read the letters before they were sent back, didn't you?" Lia wasn't sure where the sudden insight had come from. She only knew it was true.

Lucio blinked, taken back by her perception and the sudden change in conversation. "Yes, I did," he said after a long pause.

"The pain, the honesty…the determination to change things, to make them better broke my heart. I wanted, want…need changes too."

The emotions etched, entrenched in the handsome face broke hers. "I…what…how?" Lia floundered at what to say. She swallowed and waited patiently for him to continue.

"I resealed them very carefully, and then sent them back just as Gina ordered. She doesn't know I read them."

"And so, Uncle, have you? Have you changed?" Lia whispered.

"I think so."

"No more of the women Domenico accuses you of?" Lia watched her aunt put a hand to her mouth. Lucio laughed softly, not at all offended by her words or her manner.

"No. Not for a long, long time actually. You see how I live, so you understand maybe just a little why he thinks it is still going on. But no, despite not sharing a room with my wife except for the odd times she will allow it. I think I grew up finally. I don't think I have to prove anything anymore, so usually it's the bocce, if I am not working or a drink with my friends."

"Why did you stay?" Lia asked, as much for herself as for the woman listening who was wiping tears from her face, just like her husband. His hesitation had her putting the pieces together, so she pushed harder for an answer. "Why did you stay, why are you still here?" For a moment she thought he might not answer. She waited. Both women waited.

"At first because I had no place to go but then...." The silence was deafening.

"You love her!"

"Always," he answered. "It just took me a long time to understand, and I told you despite everything, she cooks, she cleans. She takes very good care of me. I am what you English, call *high maintenance,* like your mother. It takes a special person to understand this. That doesn't mean they will forgive easily, my son more so than my wife. And Lia, despite what my son thinks I would give my life for him." He shrugged, looking very lost for a moment and then he picked up his keys and left. Lia watched her aunt back away and knew this little episode was not up for discussion.

The planned visit to see Ashlee and Greg for the weekend was a godsend. Time apart could be a good thing. Lia needed to get her head around this and was grateful that she had friends of her own. A miracle, the couple were her own little miracle in this sea of emotion. Things were moving quickly and in a direction that was too exciting to miss. Lia had been the catalyst, it would appear, for much more than anyone could have bargained for. Lucio might get his wife back, Papa would get his sister back, and if he wasn't here to enjoy it, Lia was.

Lia sat at the table, her hand moving lovingly over the shiny surface, and considered the repercussions of remaining longer. Laura would not be happy, but she would accept it. Domenico would be a problem. Lia quivered involuntarily as she pictured the hard lines of his face. At times he reminded her of the military heroes featured on the covers of romance books. Short, cropped hair in severe, motionless faces, the men defied logic and managed to look unearthly beautiful despite the weapons strapped to their bodies. How would he react if things happened between his parents, and why was it, she wondered, any thoughts concerning him always sent her heart into overdrive?

Chapter 4

"**Greg just** called. He's organised the job interview at the base for today." Lia could not believe her luck. A job at the American army base, Sigonella, would make life so much more interesting. She loved Sicily, but she needed to be doing more if she continued to stay here.

"So, is this babbling you're doing supposed to interest me in any way?" Domenico asked from the recliner on the balcony.

"I need to be there quickly, so I can talk to him first, and I thought you might drive me. Please." She had no illusions about him, but she could hope, and maybe her excitement was contagious. Lia had been living here in her family's home for just over four months. Domenico however still barely tolerated her presence, even if he was a little more civil in front of his parents than times like these, where only the two of them were present.

"Please," she asked, not above begging. He just didn't understand how much she loved it here, how at home she felt surrounded by family. He disapproved vehemently that Lia had won over his mother.

"I'm busy. You get the bus from here on the days you go stay with your friends."

"It will be so much easier if you drive me, please, just this one time? Domenico? Please?"

"I'm busy." Lia bit her lip at the blatant lie. He was reading the paper. He looked up, and as always, she had to fight to not react under his piercing scrutiny. Something in his directness, the way he blatantly took in her body, what she wore and how she moved, rattled her peace of mind. At some level she accepted their bickering was safe, but right now it was all she could do not to hit him.

She blew out a breath. He had been more difficult of late, sensing the change in the atmosphere at home between his parents. Domenico hated feeling out of the loop. He didn't understand what was happening. To him it made no sense. His father had done the unforgivable and no white flag could ever be waved. He blamed Lia for the atmosphere he couldn't quite get a handle on. Lia never knew how she got inside his head, but she did. Asking him to help her had been foolish. She had just fed him ammunition for his frustrations. Yet last night he had brought home some of the sweets his mother loved and had included some for Lia. This morning he was a jerk again. Lia huffed. He smirked. Lia knew as she always did with him, that backing off achieved more, until the next round.

"Fine! I'll get the bus." She turned away and raced back to her room. If she missed this bus it would be another hour. Five minutes later she was out the door, with the sound of Domenico's laughter dogging her footsteps.

"Bus is pretty close to the stop," she heard Domenico yell, and bit back a retort.

His position gave him an excellent view of the main street and giving him the finger from downstairs would be childish. Lia knew it amused him that she wasn't above being vulgar, at least where he was concerned. Lia tugged at her hair, thinking her campaign to win back her childhood hero might have to be put to rest, buried at least six feet under.

She was perversely reluctant to let the idea go completely. In the dark recesses of her mind again, something niggled and questioned her reluctance to look further. At the moment, however when he was behaving like a complete arse, Lia wondered why she bothered to analyse things. Fuck him, she thought, as the lift sounded her arrival on the ground floor. She raced out of the apartment block.

Upstairs Domenico stood to watch her. Part of him felt bad at having refused to help her. It didn't last long. He didn't want her here. All that sweetness and light was sickening. He didn't believe the act for a second. She was Marissa's daughter, evidenced by the way she had his father wrapped around her finger. He wasn't blind to the way his friends looked at her, even Marco. *Brainless idiots, swayed by a body...* He stopped himself at that point, annoyed, because thinking about her body, or the way the bathroom smelled after she had used it, a scent so essentially Lia lingering in his memory hours afterwards, made him... He slowly unclenched his fists and deliberately changed the course of his thoughts. She was clever. She never left a thing out of place in there or in the study they shared.

Domenico considered everything she did as premeditated, calculated. It had to be. She ensured things were put back exactly the way he liked. Why did she not take the opportunity to annoy him? Lia confused him. She was so fucking perfect. Even her teeth were perfect, small and even and white although the mouth enclosing them could even make him blush when he got her started. Not that his mother ever saw that side, no matter how hard he pushed it to happen. Had his mother seriously forgotten this irritating little brat had forced her way into their lives? And what the fuck was happening with Gina and the old man now?

Domenico felt it the moment Lia looked up. Even from the distance of four floors up, their eyes met and held. She was furious. He laughed when that finger went up. She turned away as her attention was caught by the bus gliding closer. He watched as she saw her chance and darted across the road. *Stupid girl!* He knew straight away she had forgotten they drove on the opposite side of the road. He grinned, enjoying her desperation. The humour quickly disappeared when Domenico realised she hadn't seen the yellow Vespa.

"Fuck," he mouthed in English, along with other things in Italian, as the Vespa hit her. "God, damn you Lia!" Still cursing, he raced downstairs, not waiting for the lift.

There was a throng of people around her and a very apologetic rider. Like some waif Lia sat on the ground, assuring the old gentleman she was fine and that it hadn't been his fault. Her legs were grazed; her stockings torn. Her hair was not doing a good job hiding a nasty wound on her forehead, yet she was only concerned with calming the rider in that infuriatingly soft, sweet voice. He pushed past a few people standing around her and bent down in front of her, not sure of his reception, but unable to stop himself. He was partly to blame for this and the sooner he sorted it out the better.

"Oh Domenico, I missed the bus," she wailed, and then did the unexpected: held up her arms towards him.

He had an odd feeling in his chest as he bent to pick her up. He shrugged it away, just like the thought that she fitted perfectly in his arms. Carrying her back inside the building, he concentrated on trying to ignore how much he loathed the smell and look of blood. A weakness, one he couldn't control, and she was making a mess of him and his clothes with hers. This was so typical of Lia, Domenico thought, taking refuge in irritation and gritting his teeth. He couldn't enjoy a day away from work.

Unfortunately, his sense of honour wouldn't let him deny he had deliberately goaded her into being careless. She seemed small and fragile as he carried her; it triggered a faint memory. *Jesus! Trust her to turn his peaceful life into a fucking soap opera.* Something about the way she had held up her arms continued to nag at him. He opened the door, took her inside where he dumped her on the couch. She whimpered. Domenico scowled and walked to the linen press.

Grabbing the first aid kit and some towels Domenico donned surgical gloves before touching her again. Most of the injuries were on the surface, but he grimaced anyway and wondered whether she needed a doctor. All that blood was making him queasy and his face must have reflected this because she was quiet. At least she wasn't crying anymore. For some reason the tears had made him most uncomfortable. After the initial wail, the tears had petered out.

She had grazes on both legs, a deep cut of some kind on her wrist and a scratch across the side of her face just above her eye. He was worried about the dirt she had picked up off the road. After patching her up as best he could, he washed her face and wiped her legs, pulling down the ruined stockings to facilitate the process. She wore stay ups. He scowled once again as he moved the cloth up the tanned leg.

It's okay," she said suddenly, her face flushing with colour as she stared at his hand on the top of her thigh. "I should have been looking. I can finish this. Really, it's fine, but could you bring me the phone, so I can ring Greg please?"

Domenico ignored her as if she hadn't spoken, and continued the wiping movement, pushing aside the flowing fabric of her skirt and catching a glimpse of pink lace. As if sensing what he could see, Lia fiddled with the blue material, re-covering the soft smooth skin out of his sight. He continued cleaning. *Pale pink high cut lace, probably with the matching bra*, he thought and barely preventing another scowl. Sharing space in his home meant there was very little he didn't know about her. The washing drying on the balcony, told its own tale. She had good pieces: lacy, more sensual than sexy, mixed with plain, tasteful and comfortable pieces. No thongs, which he found fascinating for some perverse reason. Fuck, he couldn't believe his errant thoughts. She was a distraction. He moved away from her. His abrupt, angry movement caused her to recoil.

"I'll ring Marco," he said, trying to sound less irritated with her at the expression on her face. The cut at her wrist looked nasty. He followed the movement as she worked her top teeth over her bottom lip.

"No! It's not necessary. I'm fine, and in any case, Greg will know what do. He's a doctor too and I don't want to ruin the chance for this job." At his narrowed eyes, she added quietly, "please, just get me the phone?"

Domenico grabbed the handset and threw it at the sofa, landing beside her. She smiled her thanks and dialled. He hated her quiet dignity. It made him feel like the villain. At a profound level he knew she was genuine. *Why couldn't he just accept that and her?* He sat down beside her, glad to see the graze at her forehead had stopped bleeding.

"Thank you," she said after a brief conversation, putting her hand on his arm and handing him back the phone with her other hand. He stared at the spot where her hand and his arm met. "Greg is coming here and taking me back to the base for a few days." She quickly removed her hand.

He was relieved but not sure why. Was it the fact she had moved her hand, or that Greg picking her up meant his parents could be left out of this incident? Why did this bright, intelligent, and beautiful creature put him more on edge than any sharp knife?

"Good, in fact why don't you consider making that your home instead, or better still going home to Australia? My mother has read the damned letters; you've achieved your purpose so why are you trying to get a job?" His abruptness hurt her. This time she cringed. He didn't care. He couldn't help himself. Correction, he didn't want to help himself. Knowing he wanted her gone was enough for him. He felt the tick at the side of his mouth as she held his gaze. For a brief moment Nico was caught in the spell of a moment he didn't understand. He would have sworn she too felt it too. It flashed for an instance between them and was gone.

"And the arsehole is back." she murmured, standing up shakily. She ignored the hand he offered and limped to her room. "Fuck you!" she added for good measure, loud enough to ensure he heard.

He grinned at the language, relieved to be back in the relationship he understood. He refrained from answering. She amused him. She amused him a little too much for comfort. It got his ire up again.

"Did you forget you told your friend Laura that the arsehole looks like a Greek God just yesterday, on Skype no less?"

"With worse manners than a baboon was what I followed up with, or did you forget that part because you were too busy swaggering out in just a towel? That was pathetic even for you!"

"It didn't stop you or your friend from looking, did it? Were you hoping the towel wouldn't hold?"

"Please, of course we were. With the things I have told Laura, your arrogance being top of the list, we were hoping to see how small a dick you had. You must be compensating for something, to be so full of yourself."

"I'll get you a tape measure and let you see for yourself, although it's a little disturbing to know you have a need to discuss my anatomy."

"Do you hear yourself? Do you know how childish your behaviour is? Why would you walk out in a towel?"

"Why, you want to know why? This is my home, mine not yours. If you weren't here what I wore wouldn't matter, would it? Maybe you should take the hint? Neither I, or my anatomy, want you here."

She held her tongue and limped to her room, slamming her door as an answer to his taunts. His laugh echoed as she got herself ready. Sometimes she hated him so much she was afraid.

Chapter 5

GINA WAS insisting Domenico and Marco have her tag along. Lia now regretted coming home for the weekend. Instead of quality time with her aunt and uncle, she was being coerced into a situation she did not want. These days Lia didn't see her aunt and uncle as often as she and they liked. Lia had moved back into Greg and Ashlee's spare apartment when the amount of work she did at the navy base had increased.
"I haven't anything suitable to wear."

"We'll find something. We could cut up something of mine. I can help you."

"I don't have shoes, and that kind of dressmaking can't be done quickly." Lia replied mildly. Seven months down the track, the women now shared a relationship Lia was loath to upset or analyse. Going somewhere with Domenico however was pushing things, no matter how much Lia wanted the relationship with her aunt.

"We take the same size in shoes", Gina said, "and I wasn't always an old woman. I am sure something will suit." Lia tried not to take notice of the look on Nico's face when Gina went to her bedroom and came back with a concoction of black lace. Saturday was a ritual. Marco came for brunch, and then they would either go to the gym or a game of squash then visit Marco's parents. Both men then generally did a few hours work followed by a nightclub later that night.

Marco, she saw, was trying unsuccessfully to mask his amusement at the predicament Gina was forcing on her son. Nico liked his routine. Gina was trying to ensure his routine today would be thrown out the window. A part of Lia enjoyed the unfolding scenario despite her reluctance to go anywhere. Wisely she kept her eyes downcast, until the urge to see Nico's expression was impossible to resist, and she had to sneak a glance at the tight jaw and pursed lips. Unfortunately, she was caught by Marco, who gave her a knowing wink. The dark blond hair hung long enough to reach his collar, giving him an off-hand careless elegance to go with hazel eyes that never stopped smiling. It puzzled Lia as she scrutinised him against the other, harsher man: how someone so much fun, so charming and down to earth was Nico's best friend. Marco had been, if memory served her right, even back then so many years ago. She winked back and watched him smother a laugh as Nico looked up.

Nico, she suddenly realised, Nico; she was calling him Nico all the time now. When did that happen? She wanted to believe it a natural progression, if unsettling. Gina and Marco, depending on the conversation, almost always shortened his name. Gina distracted Lia from her musings with a pair of black suede shoes with a thin medium heel. The shoes would do; they did wear the same size. The dress was more difficult. Fully lined with three quarter length sleeves and at least one size too big meant a lot of work. The work Lia could handle, the repercussions of forced company was not so easy. But, the trouble was Gina. She was enjoying this, really enjoying it. Such a wonderful change from the grim faced and bitter woman of Lia's arrival had to be nurtured.

"Fine, you win." Gina smiled a little too smugly for Lia's liking. Lia held up the dress and studied it. Sleeves off and a little shaping to expose the shoulders, a lot of taking in, slits at the side for easier movement and it might work. The fabric was beautiful, giving Lia sudden inspiration for the shoes. Gina's excitement was contagious. She smiled back at the older woman. She started when the warmth of the moment was spoiled by the icy tremble along her spine. Nico was staring, the sneer ever-present. The hairs on her arms responded and stood on end despite the warm sunshine. The cold didn't disappear until Nico and Marco had gone.

***

Marco turned to Nico, who was retrieving the small black ball to serve again.

"What, Marco?"

"Do you have to treat her so badly?"

"I didn't say anything to her."

"Jesus Nico, you don't have to. The looks are enough on their own. Give her a break. She's lovely."

"Don't go there!"

"I'm not saying I want to fuck her!"

"Shut up Marco."

"What is your problem? So, she forced her way into your lives? Nico, look at your mother. The change is incredible. Lia is not Marissa."

Nico closed his eyes. He was thinking about the way the shower had smelt after Lia had used the bathroom the Friday morning she had arrived. The products she used were visceral. The fragrance got into his pores, followed him to work and overrode even the cloying but expensive perfume Francesca used. The one he had purchased for her. He had almost forgotten the onslaught on his senses now that Lia lived back at the base. *Liar*, he told himself. Even now, sweaty from the game and a day later, the clean fresh almost edible wisps of coconut and cinnamon were so attached to his skin, that he could barely think of anything else.

"Shut the fuck up Marco!"

"Nico, is there something more to this? She doesn't even live at the apartment anymore. She hasn't been there for almost six weeks. You're not sharing space, she's not at the dinner table and she's polite when she is visiting, unless you rile her. What's the deal here?"

Marco, Nico thought, had a point. Marco however didn't understand Lia took up space wherever she was or wasn't. "I don't like her, she annoys me. Everything about her gets under my skin. I feel displaced in my own home. Why is she still in Italy?"

"That's a mouthful and hardly fair, Nico. She wanted a family. She makes your mother happy. You don't make sense. You base your life on logic, but you can't use it with her? Don't you remember when she was a little girl? She followed you around like you were God...doting on every little thing you did. After a while none of us minded when she tagged along. She was so quiet when we were talking but funny and sweet when we gave her a chance."

"Determined, you forgot determined. And, she's not a child now!"

"No, she's not but she is still that same loving person, and after what she's been through, I understand why she came. Give her a chance."

"Can we just play ball?"

Marco nodded, letting the subject drop. With Nico you had to back off until he was ready. Gut instinct told Marco something was off. He had his suspicions. Playing ball was easier.

***

"Close your mouth, Old Man." Gina snapped, and then spoiled the effect when she grinned as he walked into the room. "Doesn't look like the same dress, does it? She is a clever one, yes?" she asked her husband.

"Lia, you look so beautiful." He paused looking doubtful. "Maybe too good, Old Woman," he said, frowning heavily. "There are some bad elements at the nightclub."

"So what, Old Man, she has the boys to look after her."

Lia really doubted that but kept quiet. She didn't want to interrupt the flow of conversation. Affection oozed in the use of *old* and in their general tone with each other.

A few times she had caught the puzzled look on Nico's, Domenico's face. Calling him Nico felt too intimate.

"Uncle Lucio, can you make two holes through the top of these shoes?"

"I'm not sure what she will do when you leave," Lucio nodded absently at Lia's request. His eyes were on Gina as she headed for the kitchen. "I'm surprised you haven't gone home already."

"Me too."

"You're not ready yet to accept he is gone."

"No, I'm not. I feel like I am waiting for something, some sign, something to stop the nightmares, something to...I don't know. It's like when something is on the tip of your tongue, but you just can't get there. I'm not ready to go and I can't explain. Besides I love the two of you. I love my job at the base and I can still help Laura online." She shrugged, and he nodded. Lia and Lucio understood each other perfectly.

Unexpected Passion

The Unexpected Series Book 2

Book 2, Unexpected Passion will centre on Alexia and Ricardo. These two strong-willed characters have more in common with each other than either one would suspect. Secrets will be revealed, and passions will surprise them both.

Although I have designed the series so that each book stands alone the books do link. I wanted the people in my novels to be a family of sorts. Alexia, the heroine of the second book is Lia's Godmother. For people with a European background a godparent is held in high esteem. Lia has an Italo-Australian background and Alexia, known as Lexi to her friends is Greek.

We don't exist in isolation and I thought it nice if we could continue learning more about Lia and Nico as the years progressed. I am hoping you like them enough to want to go back and read their story. Likewise, I will be continuing Alexia and Ricardo's story just a little in the book following theirs. In fact, it will hold a nice surprise I hope my readers will very much enjoy.

Author's note: This is still very much a raw extract and will need editing. I hope you like this enough to come back for more when I publish it early in 2019. Feel free to give me feedback on this at my email address above.

Chapter 1

Alexia Georgiou was annoyed. Too many people had time on their hands and were using it to interfere in her life. Take her friend Fran, her supposedly best friend, had just spent a full two hours lecturing Alexia on packing, the packing for her trip, not Fran's trip, but hers. Fran didn't have a bee in her bonnet, she had wasps that flapped around criticising every item Alexia had put in her suitcase. The cow had pulled everything out, tossing them all over the room. *Seriously*, Alexia thought to herself, *it was her holiday and she wanted to be comfortable. Screw Fran, screw her niece Julie and screw just about everyone else she knew.*

Lexi walked past the mirror in her lounge room, determined to ignore the hair comment as well. She got three steps past it before she stopped and turned around. It needed a cut again, and yes, she conceded to her alter ego's smug reflection, with a scowl, a colour wouldn't go astray either. *Damn it. Why won't they let me lead my own life? Why does everyone assume I need fixing? If they had kept their traps shut, I wouldn't be double guessing myself.* The person in the mirror had bags under her eyes and was carrying about six kilos more than needed, so didn't answer. *Oh! Shut up! Ten kilos, then! Are you happy now?* Alexia scowled at the reflection, furious that she couldn't lie to herself. She had a week before she took off, so a hair appointment doable if she organised herself. It might be the easy compromise to keep the busy bodies happy.

She blew out a frustrated breath because Fran had made some sense. "Fran might have had a *bit of right* on her side about the hair. The bitch!" Lexi spoke the words with a British accent and a snooty look on her face. The mirror didn't laugh. *A picture did speak a thousand words.* Lexi puffed out a whoosh of air, watching it land on the mirror as mist. Leaning in, she wiped the glass and stared at the steel grey wisps, a harsh halo against her complexion; the bits of faded colour in some of the strands long past renewable. The grey washed out the pale blue of her eyes completely, and her eyes fringed by dark lashes were her best feature. Alexia had gone grey at nineteen years of age. There had been no explanation; overnight the muddy strands of brown had acquired a greyish tinge, and the change continued until the grey dominated.

To counteract the effect sensibly, Alexia had decided on streaks. The strands of gold and reddish copper had become a trade mark, surprisingly easy to maintain, and adding a distinctive look that complemented her barely five-foot height and athletic build. Alexia had made her big breasts, small waist and nicely rounded behind work for her and had never lacked male attention, at least not till the last couple of years.

The face in the mirror had too much to say. Alexia poked her tongue at her reflection and picked up the phone. Idly she brushed her hands over the dark mahogany bookcase that sat underneath the oval mirror. Dust, she scowled again and wiped her hands on her pants. Maybe it was time she made some changes, beginning with herself. *Oh, the irony of it all!* She needed to change back to what she had been rather than change to something new.

Fuck! How did I let my nails get to this stage? It's not like I was busy dusting. She was in a rut, the worst kind – the kind where she didn't feel like doing anything. She dialled Trish's number. The woman would scream with glee, to get her hands back on Alexia's head for more than a trim. It would be like the scene from Moonstruck where Cher finally agrees to cover the grey.

Lexi hated the well-meaning conspiracy between her friends. She knew it meant she was an unappreciative bitch. She didn't care. They pissed her off because they were right. She dialled her hairdresser's number between curses. *I wonder if Trish has time to organise my nails.* Her reflection scrunched itself into a sneer.

For the first time in a long time Alexia ignored her own negativity and let herself laugh. She had to; she looked like a damned maniac.

***

Two days later and halfway around the world, Lia put down the phone, smiling. Fran had come through with the measurements she needed to complete her little project. How Fran had managed to get Alexia to agree to having her wobbly bits measured, testified to Fran's determination, proof of how much Fran cared about her friend. She had concocted some story about a party Lia and Nico were hosting during the month Alexia would stay with them in Sicily, and that Lia wanted to make her a dress as a birthday present.

A plausible enough tale, Lia thought, given Lexi had decided to extend her visit and celebrate not only her own birthday, but also the possible birth of Lia's new baby before heading home. Lia smirked on two levels; Lexi would have some unexpected additions to her wardrobe and Lia and Nico would partake in a feast of delicious Greek food. Alexia Georgiou didn't cook, she created magic.

Lexi's slump into depression after her mother's death had frightened all those who loved Lexi. Although looking after Yiayia had drained her, Lexi had idolised the woman and the loss had devastated her. Yiayia, the Greek word for grandmother and a word Lia had used since a small child, had been a loveable blend of sweetness and roguishness. The dear old thing determined early on that if Lia didn't have a grandmother of her own, she would fill that role. Yiayia, with her short-bread biscuits, had filled that role for many if truth be told including Lia's best friend Laura.

That death had come a year after the death of Lia's Papa. He and Lexi had been best friends for nearly thirty years, and Lia suspected he would have been the one to best help Lexi through the trauma. From a teenager, Lia had secretly hoped Lexi, already a mother figure, would become a more permanent part of their lives. Instead the friendship held. There were time times Lia had wondered if they had all missed something, some clue. It had never made sense to her that two people so in tune had not become more.

Lia snapped back to the present, recalling the conversation, she'd just had with Fran. Lia hated being so far away from her friends even if living in Sicily agreed with her.
Fortunately, Nico was open to visiting Sydney at any stage after the baby was born. For now, the trip meant Lexi would be here soon and Lia could smother her in as much love as Lexi would allow. Smoothing the indigo fabric and calculating how much trim she would have to buy, the sound of the door opening startled her. She tightened the belt on the jade silk dressing gown and walked out of the study.
Her heart fluttered. Moisture pooled in that special place despite the clumsiness of the huge bump on the front of her body. Or maybe it was because of the bump? *Didn't pregnancy make you too tired for sex?* Then again, not many pregnant women had a husband like hers. Lia willed her face into a bland expression. *Too late*, she thought. His beautifully cut black trousers

were tenting. She raised her brows at her husband. He laughed and kept walking the direct line to where she now stood.

"I've just had my shower. Stay away." He laughed again. *Damn the man in front of her.* She held that thought and a pout for at least five seconds. He lifted her onto the breakfast bar. He had a fetish about its height, calling it perfect for his use. Lots of furniture pieces in their home were perfect, according to Nico. "Why are you home so early? Our lunch date isn't for another couple of hours."

Nico's senses came alive at her fragrance. Arousal happened just by looking at her but when combined with coconut, cinnamon and chocolate it was impossible to reason with his cock. "My client cancelled, and I thought to myself, what can I do with the spare time? I can do some paperwork, or I could go home and spend quality time with my wife, especially when my Mamma is looking after our son."

"Damn it, you're going to mess me up, aren't you?"

"Well, if it's too much trouble I could read a book instead."

"What has reading a book got to do with the hands untying my robe..." Lia stopped talking when one of those beautifully shaped hands pushed her gently onto her back while the other wandered over the prominent belly. He bent and kissed his child before letting his lips follow a determined path.

"Nico." She whimpered as his tongue reached its target and licked the length of it.

"Do you want me to stop?"

She shook her head, too breathless to speak, and closed her eyes. The wicked instrument not only licked again but darted inside. He was slow, leisurely letting his mouth show her where his head had been all morning. She moaned, fighting the need to watch knowing it gave him a heady sense of power. Her lashes though had a mind of their own, lifting to enjoy the view, knowing full well any objections would be token.

Nico's raised brows confirmed he had been waiting for the eye contact. He grinned while his tongue continued it path to dissolve her insides. His actions were secondary. The evil man knew her well. Using her arms as leverage she raised herself onto her elbows. One hand wrapped itself in his soft dark hair. She dug her nails hard into his scalp knowing how much he relished it, his soft growls vibrating against her delicate skin. Her hormones were in permanent overdrive. His? God knew the answer to that one.

Lia tugged his hair to lift his face to hers. She barely touched his lips before he took over. He made her desperate at the best of times, but the taste of herself on his tongue scrambled her mind completely. Aggressively she thrust her tongue against his, letting him know she was ready for whatever he wanted.

Nico in turn wondered whether he would ever get enough of this woman who looked like an angel and turned into a flow of lava at his touch. He kissed her ferociously, letting the tongue that had been lapping at her essence mix with the clean fresh taste she offered. At that moment a part of him wanted her mouth on him, wanted to push his way in and fuck her mouth till he came. He craved that combined essence like a man starved for air. His impatient headstrong cock had other ideas. He kicked his pants away and let his hard length fill her.

It never failed to surprise her, this intense pleasure she received just having him inside of her. Their tongues continued to battle, mimicking the dance of body parts, pulsing and throbbing until her insides tightened, her slick softness demanding the steel rod melt against her. She moaned into his mouth as she fragmented, pushing him into his release. Sated he slumped over her, his head on her breast.

"You know," he said, his tone casual, his lips moving over her still covered nipple and breaking the quiet. "I can't decide what the man in the apartment opposite finds the most entertaining, you in this position or me without my pants."

"What? That's not possible." She cried. He grinned, and she punched at his chest, mouthing an obscenity in response to his teasing.

"What a terrible mouth you have at times. Just as well you can make better use of it at other times! You do realise he is too far across the way to see us."

"Would it bother you if he could see us?" The look he gave her made her smile. "You are a crazy perverted man. "
"You have to admit, there's a lot worthwhile to see."

His tone sent those little shivers back into play. She watched as he slid out of her and used the dressing gown to wipe himself, and then do the same for her. She punched him again for good measure.

"Lia," he asked, suddenly losing the humour in his face and moving one hand to her throat. He applied the smallest amount of pressure.

She waited quietly. When he did that it was because he felt overwhelmed. Since he had accepted she was having this second child, he had moments when he needed to exert control. He felt he had power over her this way, or so he thought. Lia let him believe it. Some people might not understand. They had no idea of how his mind worked. Lia did. His thumb made small circles at the base of throat. Still he said nothing. He took a breath, taking her hand with his, he used the thumb of that hand to rub lightly over her engagement ring. She wondered if he knew that his left thumb was imitating his right one.

"How did you know this was the ring I wanted you to choose?"

Careful not to react to the strange way his mind worked, she let out a small sigh at the question almost three years overdue. That meant three years of thinking about it, three long years. She smiled gently and turned to him as if he had asked a perfectly simple question. "Nico, it was a square ruby, with two small square diamonds. The symmetry was perfect, the stones were bold, and the ring combined yellow and white gold. It suited us both. Of course, it would be the one you wanted. It was perfect." She crinkled her nose at him. "I imagine Seppo would have received some very exact instructions. And, I'm not surprised he could fill them. His store was full of things that would appeal. You're his landlord, aren't you?" She raised a brow and he flushed slightly. She lifted her fingers to his cheek and he leaned in, letting her soothe him. "Nico, I know who you are."

"Yes, you do. Why?"

She didn't answer, knowing full well he wasn't ready yet. His silence indicated his own awareness of the fact. His hand continued the small caress at her throat before lifting her off the table, his face re-arranging itself to the relaxed man who had come home early just to make love to her. She bent down to pick up his things.

"Don't. Leave them," he whispered against her ear. He inhaled her fragrance as she tightened her arms around his neck and put her cheek against his. He liked that he didn't have to explain himself.
"Did you sort out Alexia?"

"Yes, I did. I have some bits and pieces to finish she doesn't know about in time hopefully in time for you to deliver when you fly to Rome. I'm confident I can."

"Good." He kissed her as swung her into his arms carry her to their bedroom. "No reason then not to concentrate on your husband."

Chapter 2

"*Where was the sign?*" There was supposed to be, a sign somewhere and Alexia Georgiou refused to take her medication in response to the agitation knocking at her mind. Anxiety had been her enemy too long. She would not panic. *She could speak the language and she was a mature person, fifty-four years old, and surely this counted for something? That's damn right. I won't panic.* She stopped to look around her reminding herself to breathe, to stay calm. Lia's friend Annalisa had seemed very efficient in all their conversations, she reassured herself.

The airport, big, noisy and so busy disconcerted her after the smoothness of the trip. *I've got to get a grip on myself, stop this infernal shaking and I'll be fine. Oh God, I've also got to stop talking to myself out loud. Shit, starting now.* She ignored the look the woman gave her but then found herself relenting. The woman recognised a case of nerves and the look appeared genuinely sympathetic. Lexi gave a small shy smile. The smile she received in return bolstered her along with the woman's words. "Tutto á posto?"

"Si, grazie." A stranger asking her if all was well settled her nerves. Lexi turned with more determination. After all she had been to Italy before even if that had been a different time with less people crowding around. She had succumbed to superstition many years ago and thrown a coin into the Trevi Fountain, several coins, and they had brought her back. Maybe magic existed. Lord knew she could use some.

That was the real problem, not the crowed Rome airport, but the realisation that somewhere along the line over the last few years she had run out of the energy to believe in anything. The smallest things unnerved her, overwhelmed her including this trip. Acknowledging it as a good idea, didn't make it easier to be here. She wished it did because she certainly needed to relax and enjoy life again. She needed to push the panic down and keep it from ruining every experience. Breathing deep she reminded herself that travel meant adventure, a chance to find the *fun Lexi* again.

"Signorina Georgiou?" The voice, rich in tone in the way of Italian men, had a delicious accent giving her Greek name a European class which Alexia relished. Maybe her determination to embrace good vibes would pay off. She felt tingly at the timbre of his greeting. Turning to face the voice, that view was quickly challenged. The man in front of her crushed all positive thoughts and brought Negative Nellie back to the surface.

The man had yellow-brown eyes in a tanned face, cat's eyes. *Did that make sense? Did people have yellow eyes?* He frowned. *Oh shit, did I say that aloud? Too bad!* Lexi continued her slow perusal. The man remained silent. Long dark, dirty-dark blonde hair tied back in a pony tail, greeted Lexi along with an earring in his left ear and an almighty sleeve of a tattoo, or did people call it a tattoo sleeve she wondered? It started at the wrist and climbed its way past the biceps on his right arm. The thing looked like a rose bush, a climbing rose decked in glorious pinks against a green-leafed backdrop.

Lexi had to admit, it had a certain charm, could be termed beautiful not that she liked tattoos, well maybe smaller ones. Surprisingly the bevy of roses added to the aura of alpha masculinity. Those tiger eyes made sure of that. He was wearing a white T-shirt, spoiled in her opinion, by the evil glare of the black skull emblazed across the chest area. She couldn't help it. Her nose wrinkled, her lips pursed unpleasantly as she continued her perusal. The man had on very well-fitting blue jeans totally ruined by the rip on one thigh and the several smaller rips on the knee and calf of the other leg. Unfortunately for her he was also wearing a badge that identified him as Ricardo from 'Paradiso Tours".

"Fuck! You have to be kidding me!" Alexia whispered, under her breath. *It was supposed to be under her breath but judging from his reaction it may have been a teeny bit louder than that.* The polite interest he had been displaying inched up a notch. There was a sudden gleam in the golden eyes that she couldn't quite read but she knew enough to know it didn't reflect well on her. The tilt of his head announced only too well that he meant it as a superior look. Now he was the one perusing her outfit, her, Flattering was not in the vocabulary of his piercing eyes.

Ricardo, she knew instinctively, was thinking the old bag had a few problems with the way she saw the world. His eyes, expressive and narrowed, branded her as one of those people that judged the surface instead of the person underneath. She felt it and he couldn't be faulted for it. She did, him at least. Normally a pragmatic person, Lexi accepted rather than judged. The last few years tolerance had taken a beating but her reading of people had remained.

Lexi swore she could see and feel his mind working to put the thoughts together. Lexi had spent too many years in a classroom with too many varying personalities not too recognise *the look*. The conversation in his brain went like this - of course he had to be the odd one, not her in her regulation navy track pants, matching zippered jacket and tourist running shoes. Lexi could feel the distain. Hell, she could practically taste it and for once Alexia wished with all her heart she wasn't so good at reading people. Her honesty screamed the fault as her own.

Defensive, she had judged him. He had reacted accordingly. *Why the hell did she care, what he might be thinking anyway*? Pulling herself together and settling her features into a neutrally pleasant expression, an oxymoron she knew, Lexi offered him her hand. The grip was strong and surprisingly warm. To his credit he recognised that she had had read him and he rearranged his features into a friendlier, more welcoming look but the gleam in his eyes remained. He found her amusing.

Of course, this could also be just a conversation in her head and he might not be thinking anything. No, Alexia knew better. This man had hidden layers despite the hippie look. *Did people still say hippie, or did 'out there' fit better?* Either way, he was too old to dress like that. *Was he even a real Italian? Weren't they all well-dressed, smooth and charming by nationality?* She dug deep into her memories of her first time in their country and she was positive it had been different.

This guy looked like he should be on a surfboard at the beach or in a rock band, not representing some fancy tour company. *To be fair, his age negated the rock band notion even if things these days were more relaxed. He had to be in his fifties. Well, that didn't bode too well, did it? Damn!* Lexi did not find the idea of being stuck on a six-week tour with a 'wanabee-young', middle-aged flower-child instead of a professional. She'd bet a lot of money on the fact that bimbos were his favourite hobby. *What the hell?*

Ricardo was trying not to let his feelings show. His amusement lessened the more those lips of hers disappeared into that fake almost-smile. This was so typical of this generation of female no matter where they came from, always so ready to judge on appearance as if she could talk. *Pazienza, Ricardo*, he told himself as he repeated his question to her again. He needed an acknowledgement about her bags. Maybe he should let her have her fill of looking, at his arm, his hair, his earing and yes, the arm again. *Ma dai, ancora con questo sguardo? Get over yourself lady!* Pointedly he looked down at her luggage and back up at her face hoping to snap her attention back to his question. "Is this all you have?"

"Yes. Yes, it is." She hated sounding rattled. His fixed gaze though unnerved her. She felt measured and found wanting. Mind you, who didn't these days? Ridiculous to start her trip in this manner, with this man she barely knew. There she went again, feeling sorry for herself. Hadn't she just made up her mind to relax?

"Good. Follow me please," he said firmly, making sure he had her attention, and kept it.

She nodded, feeling a little silly, as he grabbed the blue suitcase. He led her back to the small transit vehicle. She saw three possible couples and two elderly ladies all chatting excitedly together. "Fuck! They're all American! Geez Fran, you should have come with me. This is a nightmare," she exclaimed hearing their accented voices and bit her lip as Ricardo glanced back at her. She needed a filter big time for her mouth, or at least she needed to concentrate on thinking things in her head and not saying them out loud. But come on, nearly all the people she knew that had taken tours in Europe, had warned her about loud whining Americans, so she could be forgiven for reacting the way she did.

He, Ricardo obviously disagreed, and thought her the problem. *Shit, she was the problem. Hadn't she gone off her head at the very people who had said that? Great. She was being a real cow, a judgemental bitch. Yellow eyes thought so, and she couldn't blame him. What the hell was wrong with her?* She had agreed to all of this. Ricardo, of Paradiso Tours, had every right to raise those brows, and give her that look.

The chatting had stopped. Curious and friendly smiles came her way as she boarded. She surmised the only one to have heard her little outburst was the blonde bozo. *Lucky for me!* Lexi winced, feeling awkward enough without her mouth antagonizing people before the tour even started. She smiled back and sat down quietly fiddling with her small backpack. She didn't know whether she could do this. She wasn't ready for all these people. Alexia didn't know what was worse, her fear or the battle to keep it hidden. The golden hues had darkened to a deep brown and were staring at her in the rear-view mirror. She cringed further inside her head. Her shoulders followed suit as she realised he didn't like her and wasn't hiding it behind a polite mask. It wasn't good business but at least he was honest.

Emotions in Evolution (an extract)

I hope you enjoy a glimpse into my new poetry book **Emotions in Evolution**. Along with some longer pieces I have focused on something different. During my writing travels I have fallen in love with the haiku and the cinquain, two very beautiful poetry mediums. In this book I explore them a little, with a focus on nature and colours. Plants and colours have their own meaning and it was challenging working with this.

Swimming in deep water

I float;

my face uplifted.

I drown;

the water shifted.

The pull was strong

and called my name.

I recognised a siren song

from whence it came

but I am not

confident.

I failed to fight.

I am not yet

solvent

and am blinded by light.

I am a weak human creation.

I truly do my best

to ignore the clawing sensation

as I fail each test.

To survive you must make the dive.

That's right, isn't it?

The day to thrive will arrive.

That's true, isn't it?

Natural Inspiration

Around me,

surrounds me.

For there is magic

filling my pores,

taking over my senses

on the green hued floor

of sprouting leaves and roots,

inside stick-like branches

and in natural lawns

of fresh smelling and smiling fields.

I seek their calm.

I am avarice for the peace

of different shades that

blend beckoningly, battling

the never ceasing contrasting

seams of bounty the humans only lease.

I seek possession.

I am anxious for title deeds,

for proving ownership

and having rights, and

to reach ruin without replenishing.

Quiet! I hear voices, a question!

Did someone call Earth a rental?

Cinquain and the Hibiscus

Divination

Chaotic, random

Lusting, loving, repelling

Fertile five petal protection

Hibiscus

Cinquain and colour

Yellow

Impatient, vibrant

Stimulating, creating, investigating

Bringing clarity to the mind

Sunshine

Orange

Sociable, playful

Rejuvenating, self-indulging, overbearing

Stimulating appetite and conversation

Optimism

Colour me Blue in Haiku

wet waves rippling

muddy grey to ocean blue

salt encrustation

white softness

bubbles in the wide grey blue horizon

Until next time
Barb 2018

www.ingramcontent.com/pod-product-compliance
Lightning Source LLC
Chambersburg PA
CBHW031415290426
44110CB00011B/390